Map Legend

Borders

Country border

Natural Park border

Military/restricted area

Fence

Gate

Roads & Paths

Surfaced roads

Dirt roads & tracks

Walking trails

Restricted/guided trails

Obligatory walking direction

Major hiking/trekking routes

Downhill skiing routes & lifts

Natural Terrain

Lakes, ponds

Rivers; streams

Waterfalls

Wetland

Wood

Scrub

Heath

Meadow; grass

Sand; beach

Glacier

Crevasse

Cliffs; rocks; arete

Scree; shingle

Viewpoint

Cave entrance

Man-made Features

Farmland

Orchard

Power line

Railroad

Pipeline

Quarry

Monument, tourist attraction

Cemetery

Amenities

Rangers post

Police station; border control

Tourist information

Hotel, hostel

Guest house; alpine hut; shelter

Established campground; also staffed, commercial or otherwise regulated campsite

Closed campsite

Hospital

Post office

Playground

Transportation & Transport Amenities

Car parking

Bus station/hub

Bus stop

Ferry & cruise ship routes

Airport

Food

Cafe, restaurant, bakery

Grocery store; supermarket

All Elevations are in Meters

Mercator Projection

Sergio Mazitto Tourist Topo Maps

Available from
Amazon.com and other retailers

Marcayphiri

Habaspampa

Pampallacta

Pampallacta

3000

2900

2800

2800

Río Tancac

Río Urubamba

Tancac

Phiry

8535000

8535000

Kamicancha

Chicobamba

Nunaypata

Canaquillca

Huayrajpunko

Bandolista

CU-10

Río Patacancha

Juchuy Paques

2900

Rumira

Intihuatana

Bandolista

Parón

Pacpayoc

Chimpachacra

Cachiccata

Muyopata

San Isidro

Parking.Cochera. (informal)

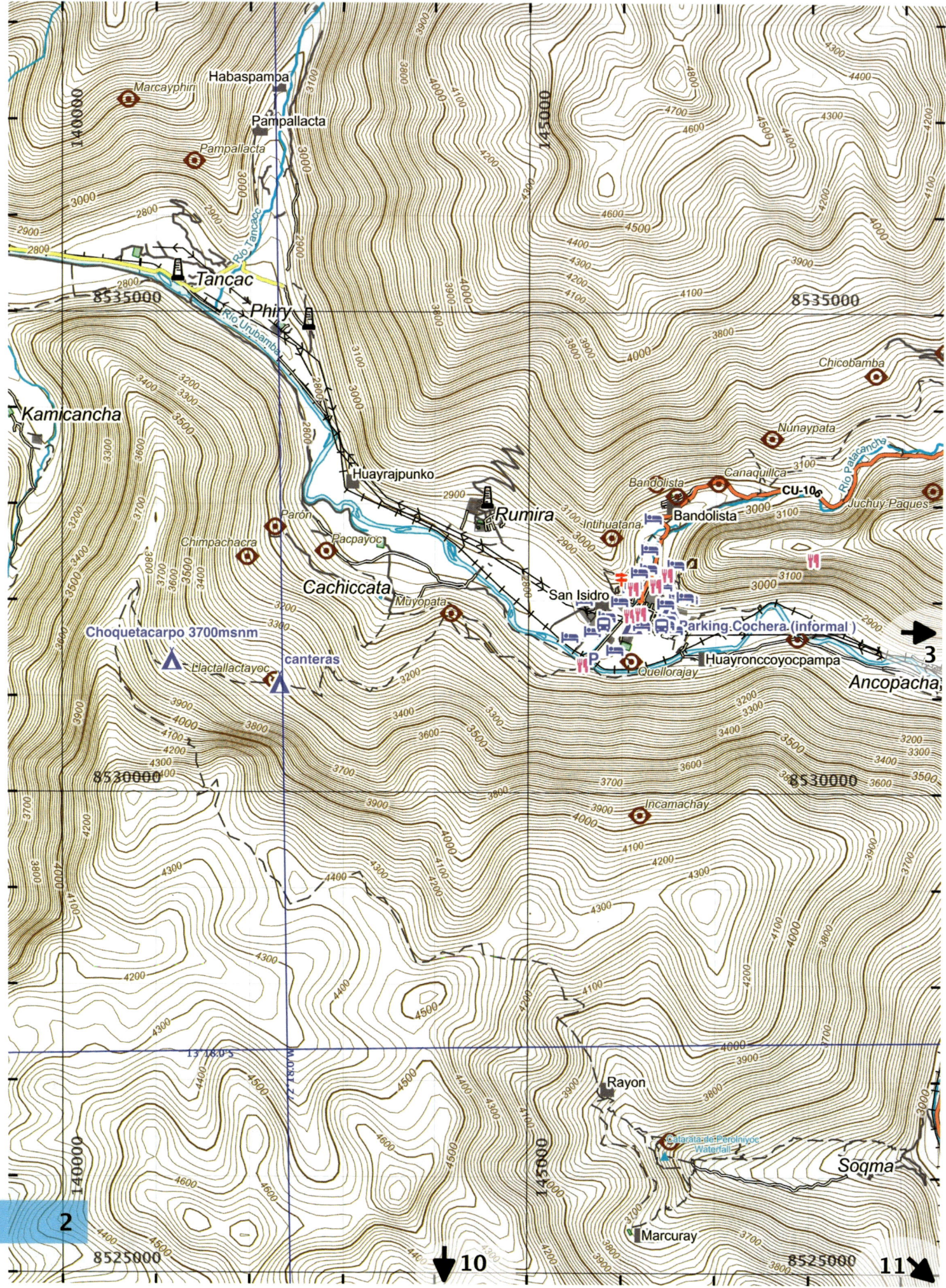

Choquetacarpo 3700msnm

canteras

Llactallactayoc

P

Quellorajay

Huayronccoyocpampa

Ancopacha

3

8530000

8530000

Incamachay

13 18.0 S

Rayon

Catarata de Perolniyoc
Waterfall

Soqma

Marcuray

8525000

8525000

10

11

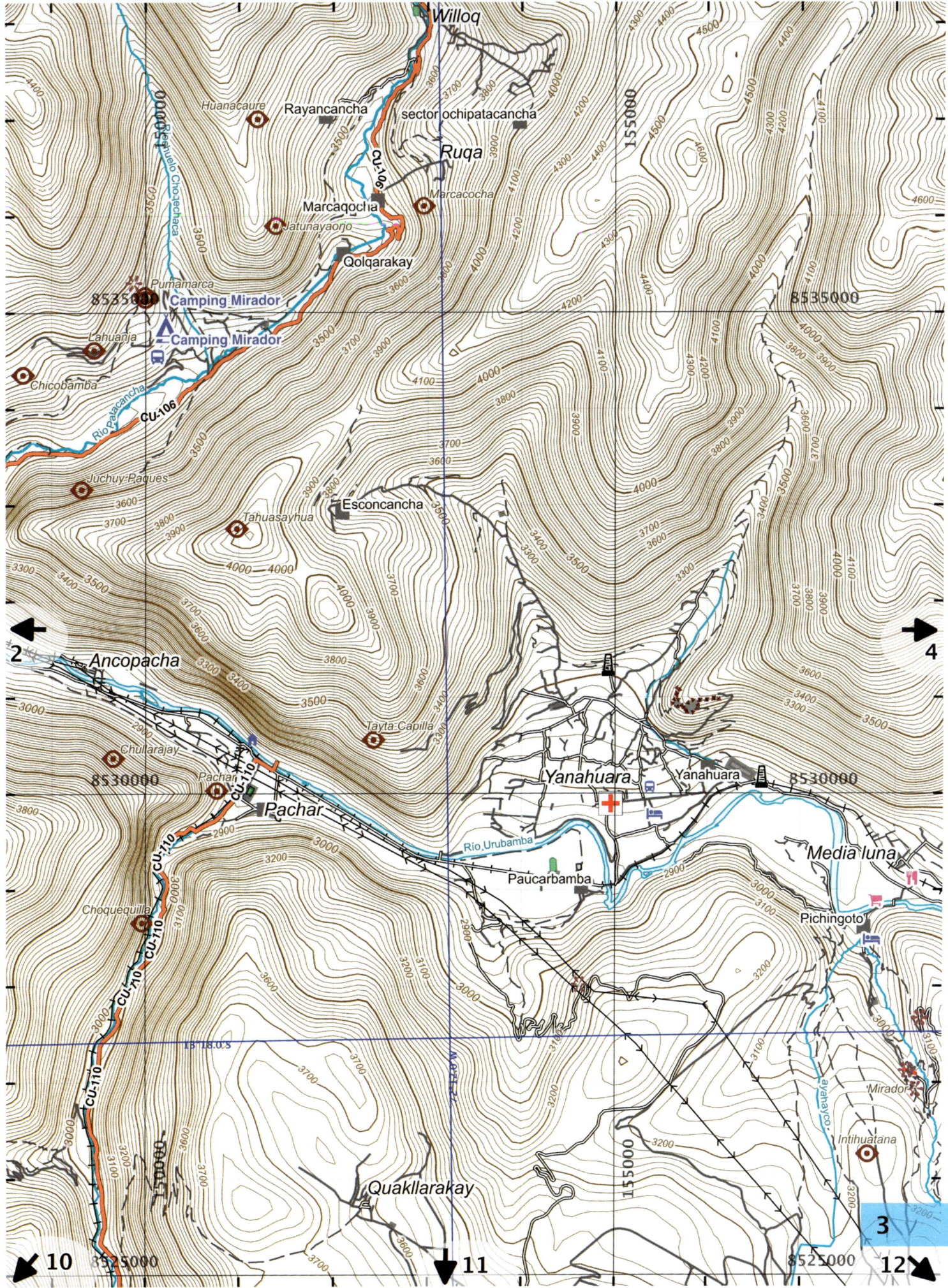

Willoq

Huanacaure

Rayancancha

sector ochipatacancha

Ruqa

Marcacocha

CU-106

Marcaqocha

Jatunayaorjo

Qolqarakay

Pumamarca

Camping Mirador

Camping Mirador

Lahuania

Chicobamba

Río Patacancha

CU-106

Juchuy Paques

Tahuasayhua

Esconcancha

Ancopacha

Chullarajay

Pachar

CU-110

Pachar

CU-110

Tayta Capilla

Yanahuara

Yanahuara

Media luna

Choquequilla

CU-110

Río Urubamba

Paucarbamba

Pichingoto

CU-110

ayahuayco

Mirador

Intihuatana

Quakllarakay

8535000

8535000

8530000

8530000

8525000

8525000

155060

155000

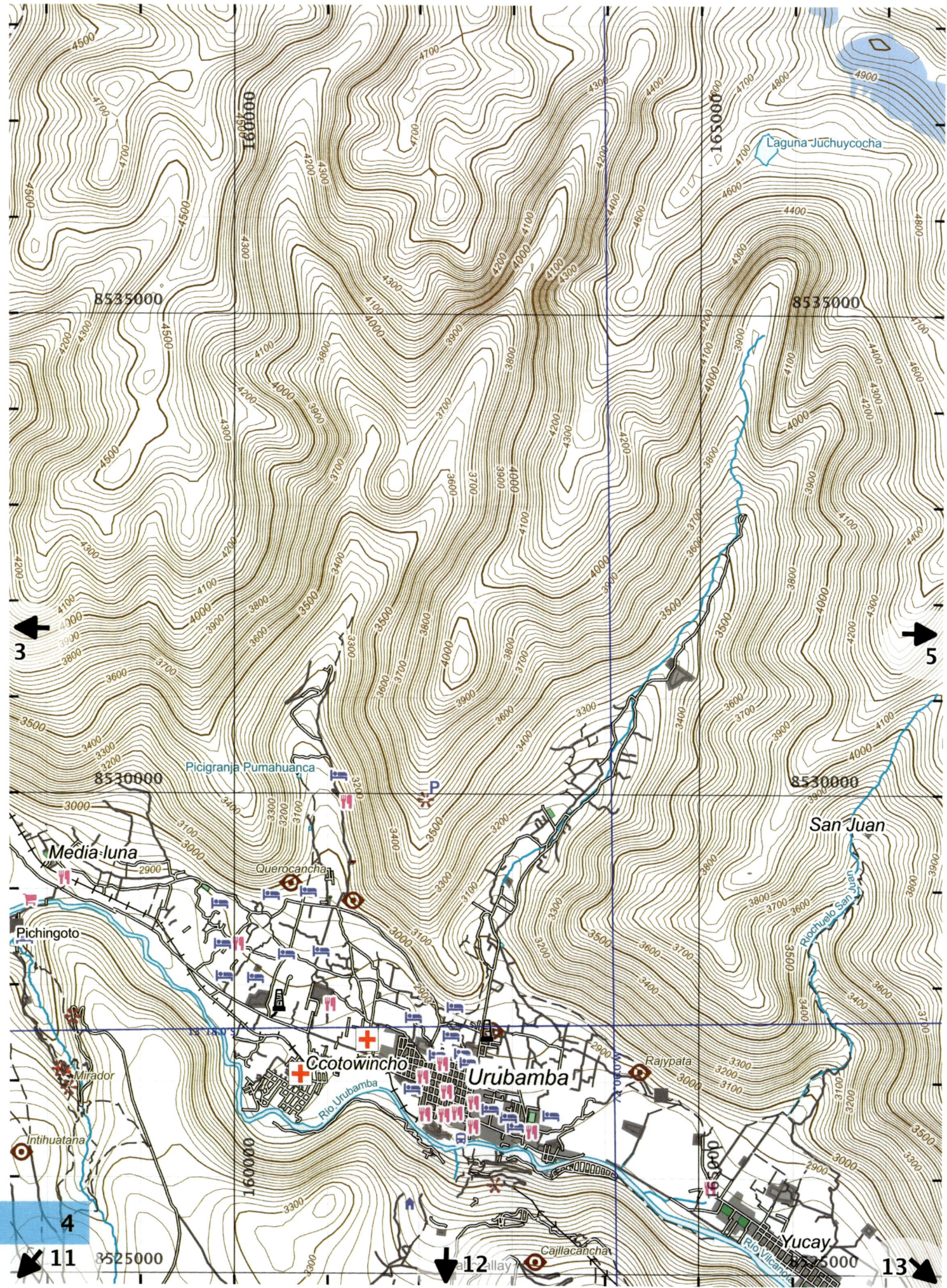

Laguna Juchuycocha

8535000   8535000

3
5

Picigranja Pumahuanca

8530000   8530000

P

San Juan

Media luna

Querocancha

Pichingoto

Mirador

Ccotowincho

Rajypata

Urubamba

Río Urubamba

Intihuatana

4

11   8525000
12

Cajllacancha

Yucay

Río Vilcanota

13

Chicón
5530

5280

5100

San Juan

Riachuelo San Juan

Yanacocha

Little Falls
Waterfall

Big Falls
Waterfall

Mirador

Huaran

Arin

Campo Verde Pitusiray

Sillacancha

Río Vilcanota

Leonchayoc

170000

175000

8535000

8535000

8530000

8530000

8525000

8525000

5

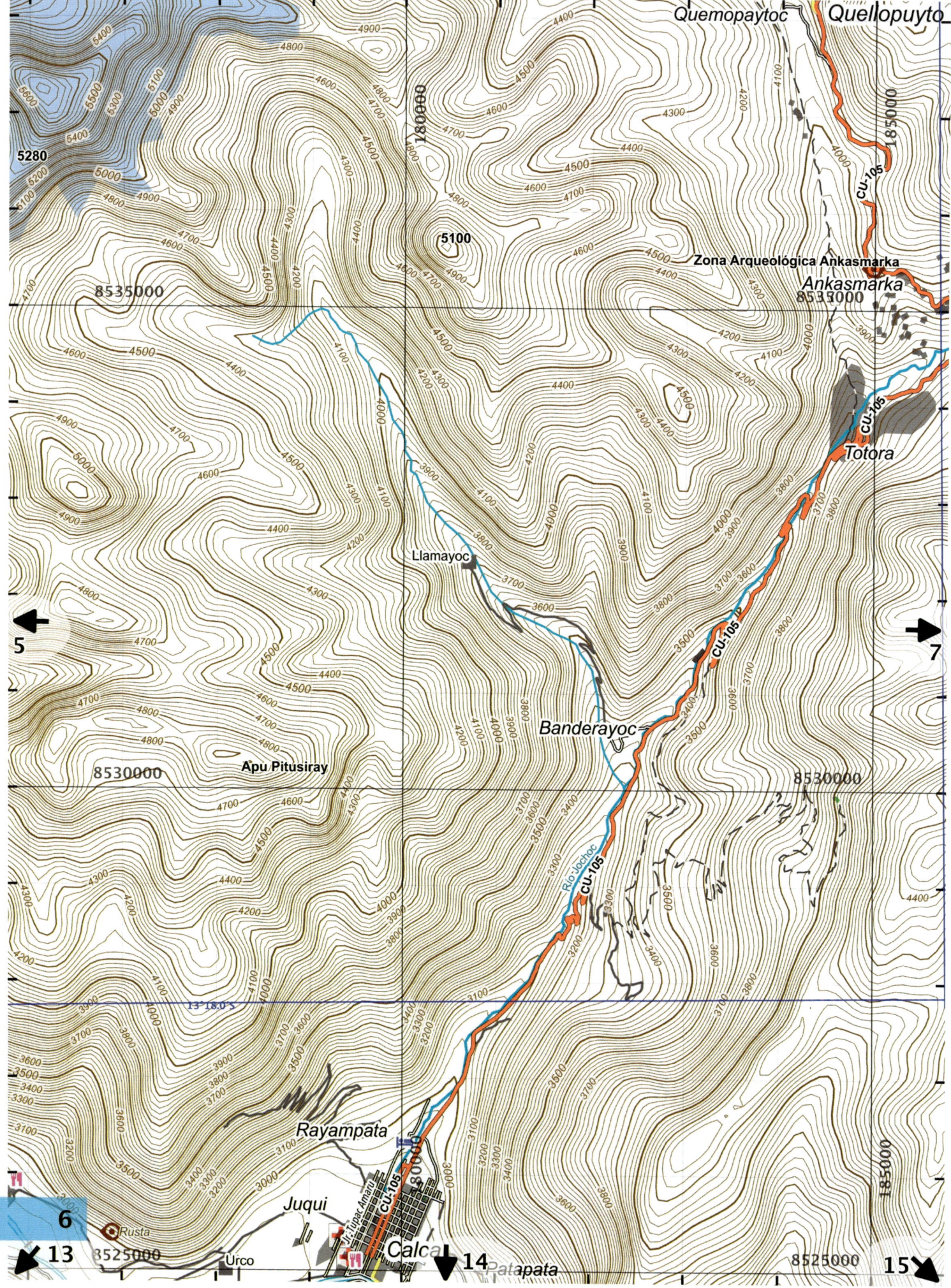

5280

5100

CU-105

Zona Arqueológica Ankasmarka

Ankasmarka

8535000

8535000

Totora

CU-105

Llamayoc

CU-105

5

7

Banderayoc

CU-105

Apu Pitusiray

8530000

8530000

Río Jochoc

CU-105

13°18.0'S

Rayampata

CU-105

Juqui

V. Tupac Amaru

CU-105

Calca

6

13

8525000

Rusta

Urco

14

Patapata

15

8525000

Zona Arqueológica Ankasmarka
Ankasmarka
CU-105
CU-105
Río Jochoc
CU-105

8530000

8530000

Sapacto

CU-597

CU-597

CU-597

13 18.0 S

CU-597

Ttio

CU-597

Sayllafaya

CU-597

CU-597

CU-597

CU-597

CU-597

Illmito

Lanza Cancha

Río Cancomayu

Tojra

195000

200000

8535000

8535000

8530000

8530000

8525000

8525000

13°18.0'S

71°48.0'W

7

9

15

16

17

8

Challabamba

Parcco

Llajtajolloy

Pucara

Puquio Tocyac

8535000

8530000

8525000

CU-597

9

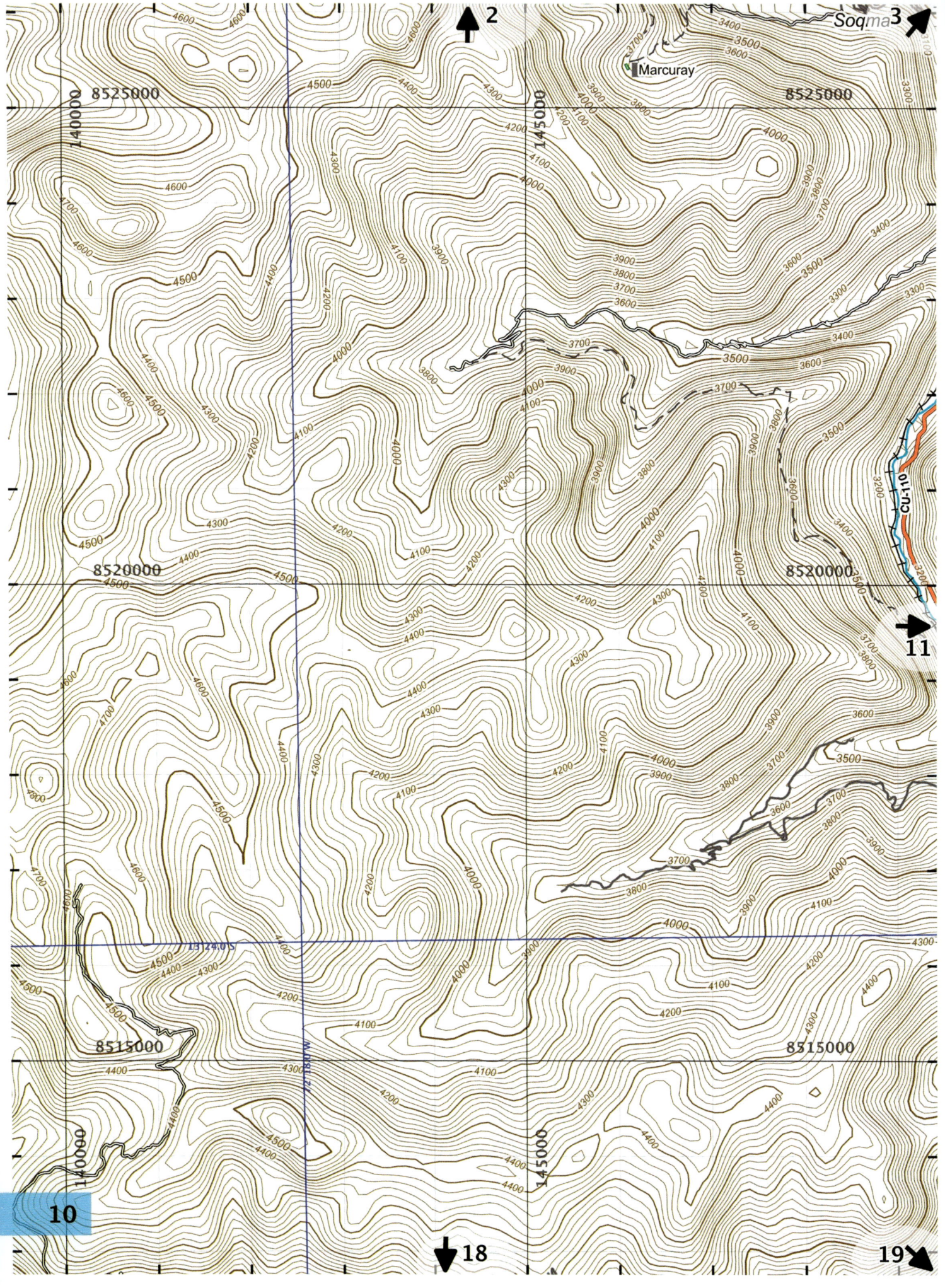

Soqma

■ Marcuray

8525000
8525000

8520000
8520000

11

8515000
8515000

10

18

19

CU-110

140000

145000

140000

145000

4600
4500
4400
4300
4200
4100
4000
3900
3800
3700
3600
3500
3400
3300
3200
4700

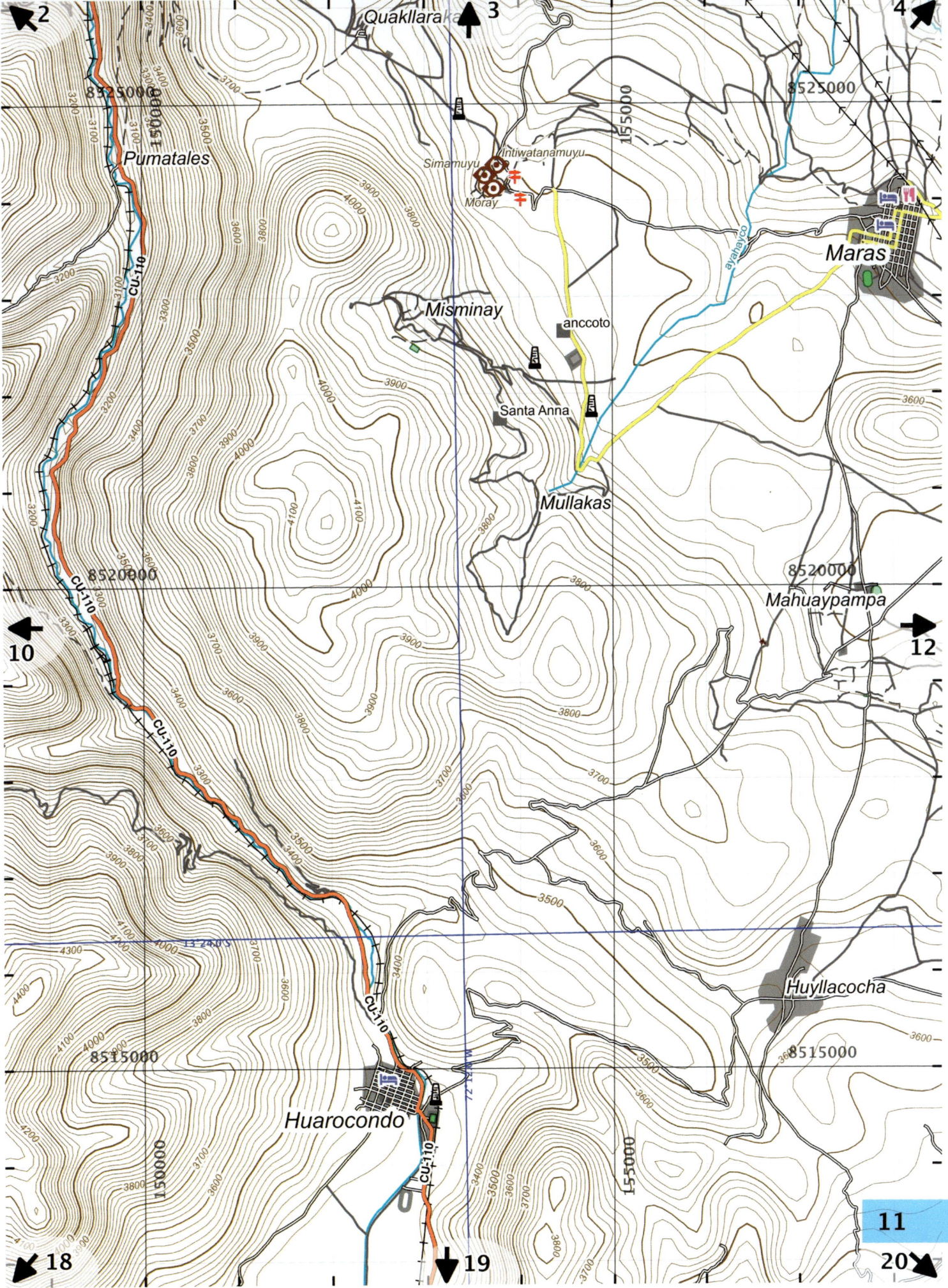

Quakllara

8525000

155000

8525000

Pumatales

Simamuyu

Intiwatanamuyu

Moray

Misminay

anccoto

Maras

CU-110

Santa Anna

ayahayco

8520000

8520000

Mullakas

Mahuaypampa

CU-110

CU-110

13 24'0''S

Huyllacocha

8515000

8515000

155000

150000

CU-110

CU-110

Huarocondo

M. WAY 7L

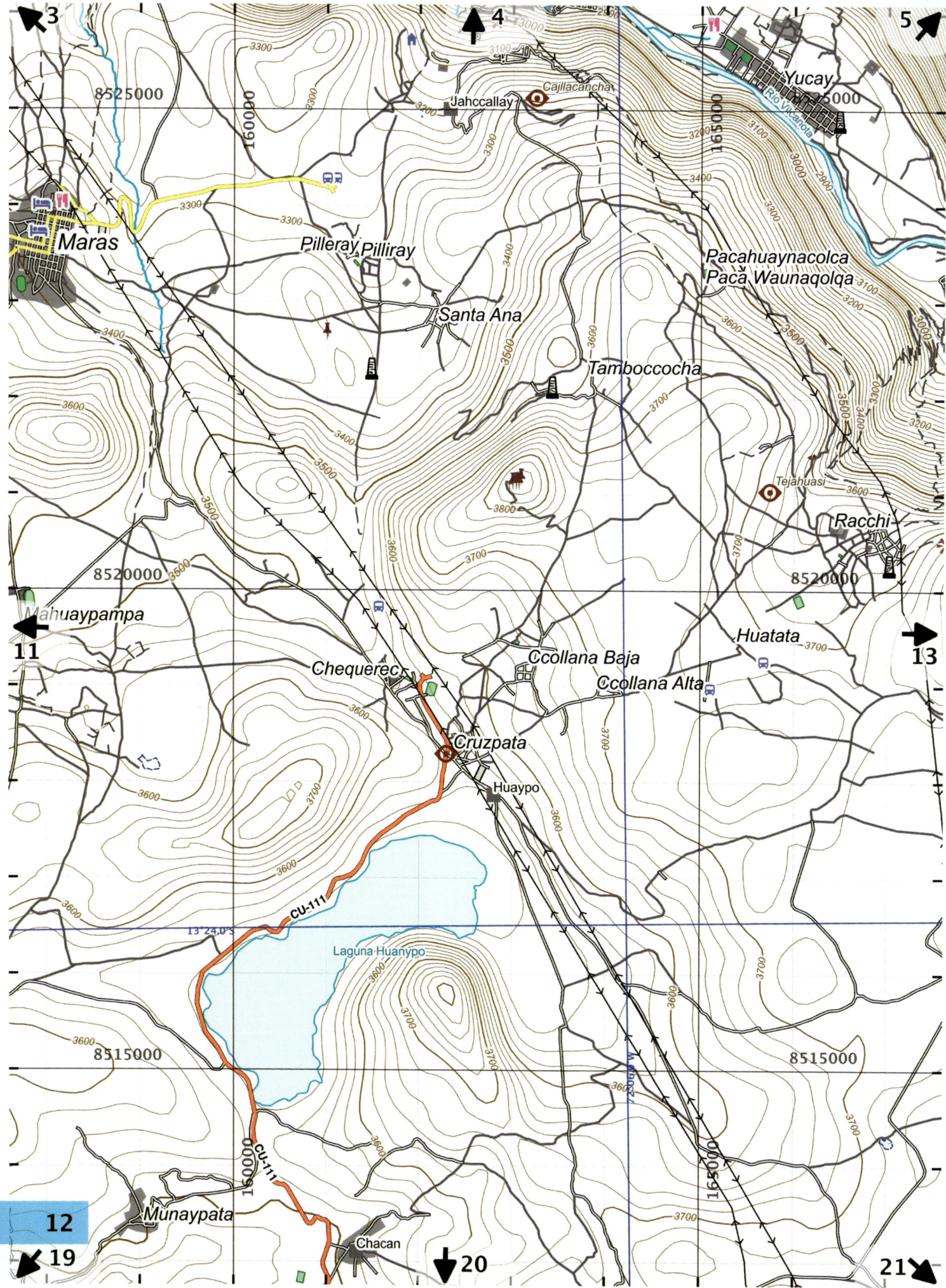

8525000

Yucay

Río Vilcanota

Jahccallay

Cajllacancha

Pilleray Pilliray

Pacahuaynacolca
Paca Waunaqolqa

Santa Ana

Tamboccocha

Tejahuasi

Racchi

8520000

8520000

Mahuaypampa

Huatata

Chequerec

Ccollana Baja
Ccollana Alta

Cruzpata

Huaypo

CU-111

13°24.0'S

Laguna Huanypo

8515000

8515000

CU-111

Munaypata

Chacan

Maras

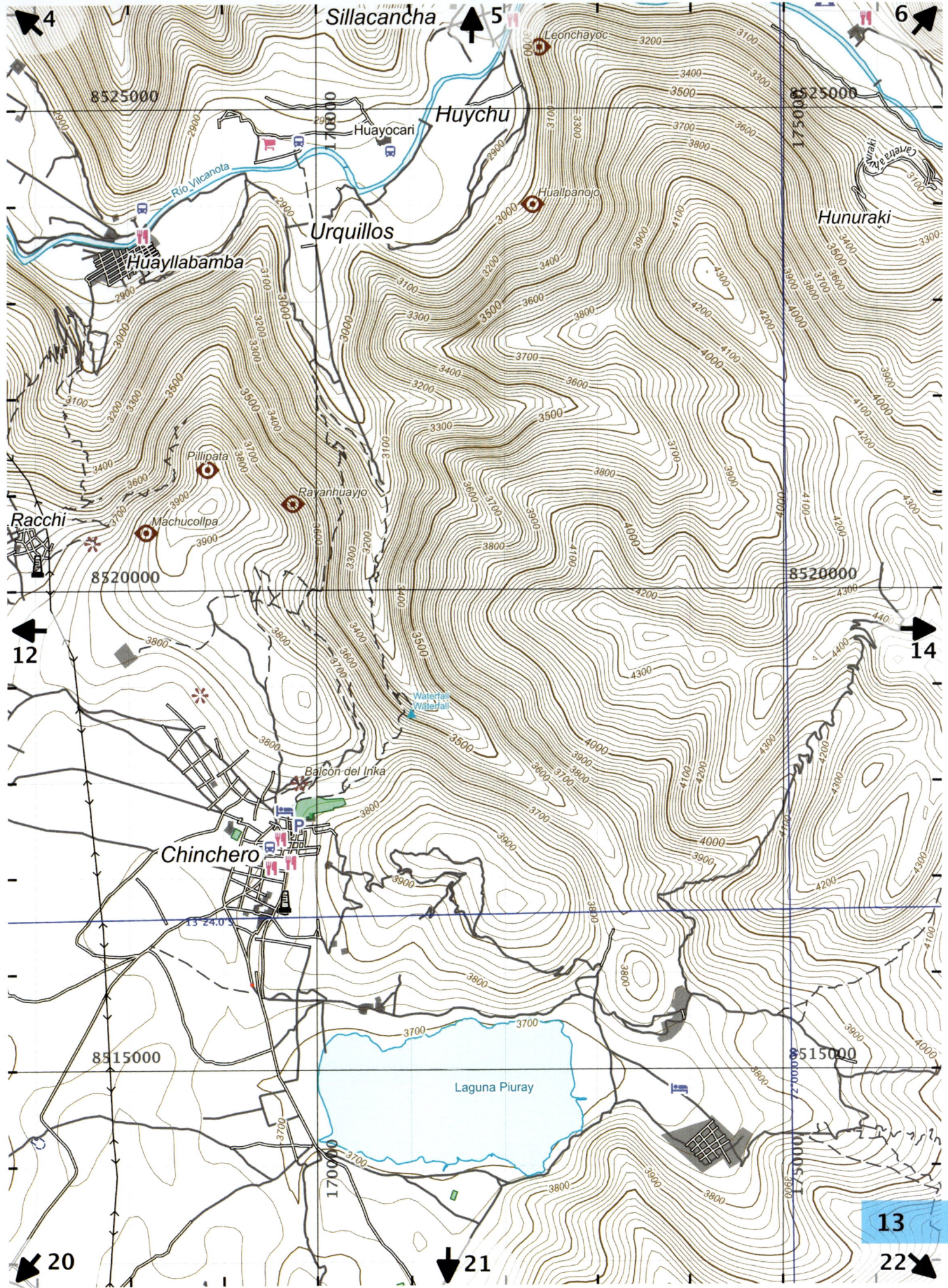

Sillacancha
Leonchayoc

8525000

Huychu

Huayocari

Huallpanojo

Hunuraki

Río Vilcanota

Urquillos

Huayllabamba

Pillipata

Racchi

Rayanhuayjo

Machucollpa

8520000

Waterfall
Waterfall

Balcon del Inka

Chinchero

13 24.0 S

8515000

Laguna Piuray

13

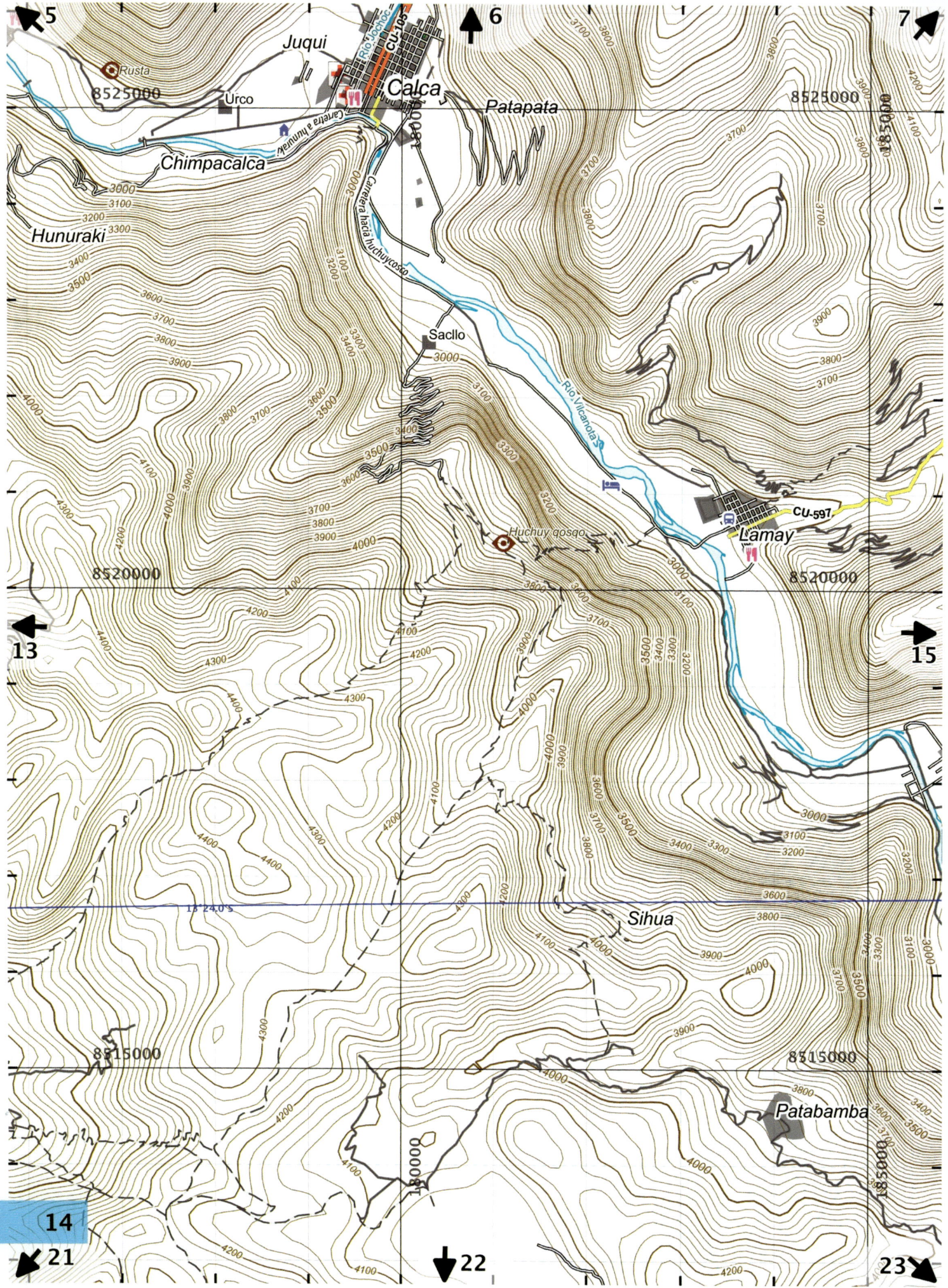

Juqui

Calca

Rusta

8525000

8525000

Urco

Patapata

Chimpacalca

Hunuraki

3000
3100
3200
3300
3400
3500
3600
3700
3800
3900

Sacllo

Río Vilcanota

Huchuy qosqo

Lamay

CU-597

8520000

8520000

4100
4200
4300
4400

18 24.0 S

Sihua

8515000

8515000

Patabamba

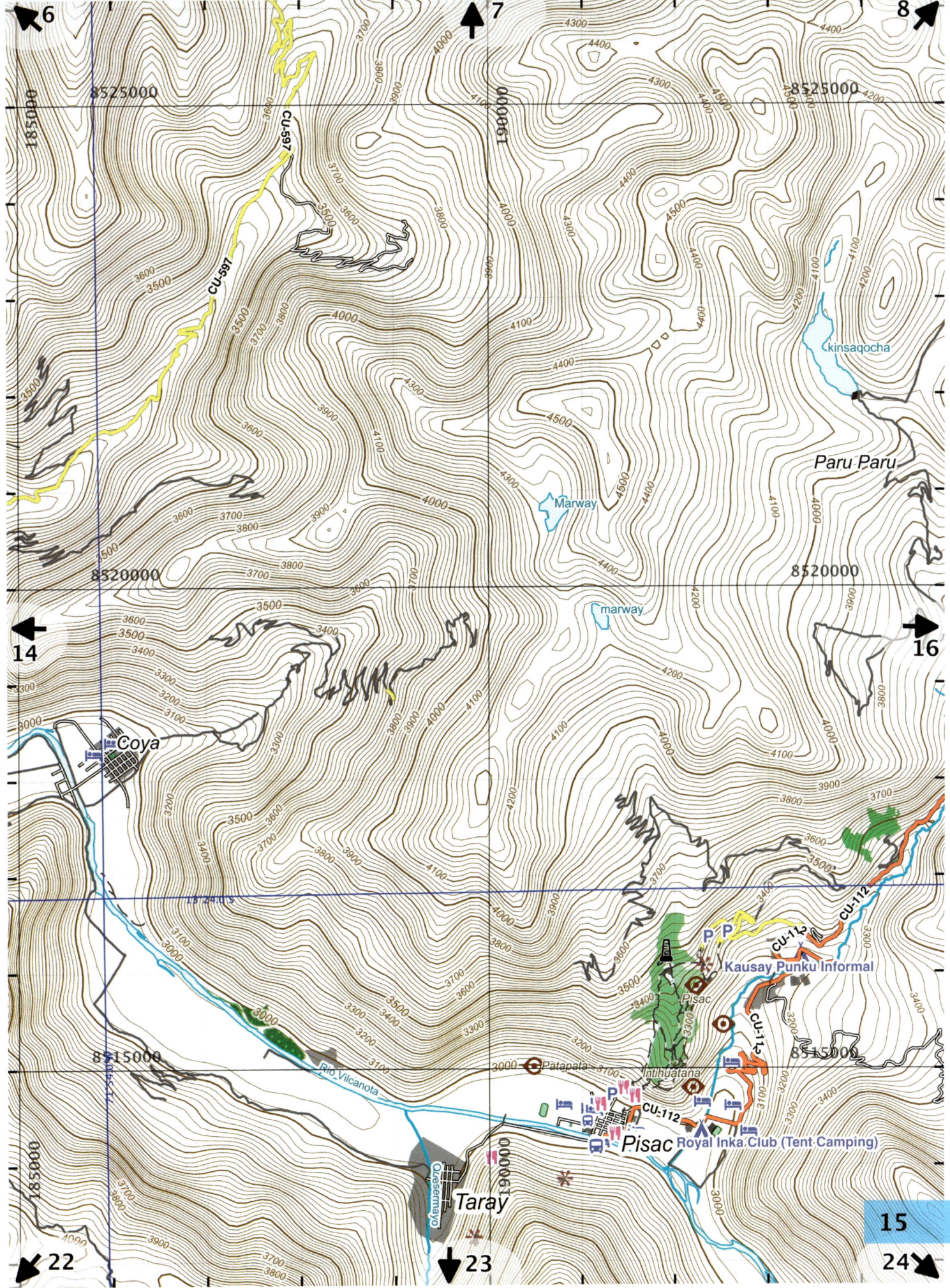

8525000
8525000

CU-597

CU-597

kinsaqocha

Paru Paru

Marway

marway

8520000
8520000

Coya

Rio Vilcanota

8515000
8515000

Patapata

Intihuatana

Pisac

Kausay Punku Informal

CU-112

CU-112

CU-112

CU-112

P P

P

Pisac

Royal Inka Club (Tent Camping)

Quesermayo

Taray

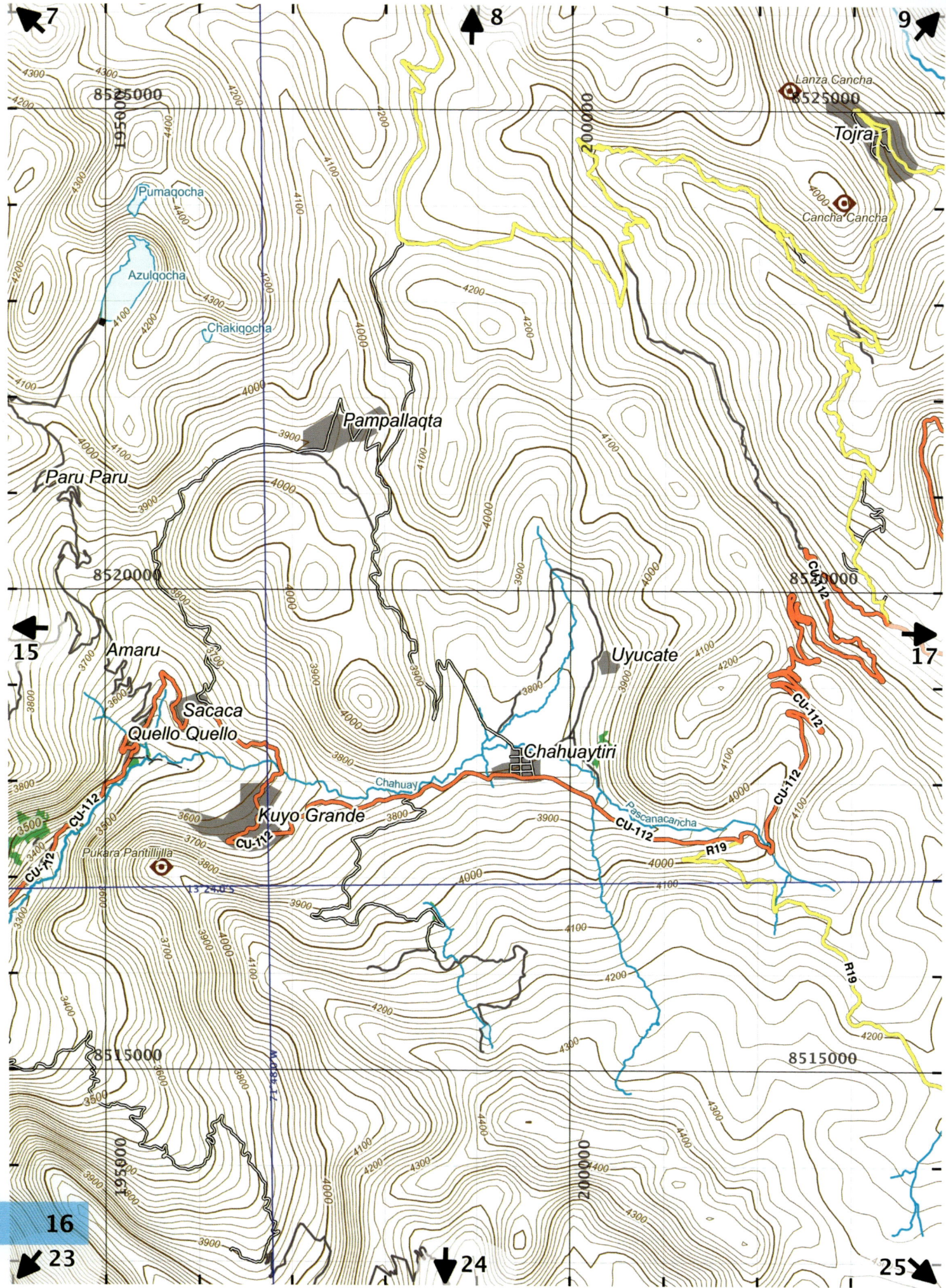

8525000

200000

Lanza Cancha

8525000

Tojra

Pumaqocha

4000

Cancha Cancha

Azulqocha

Chakiqocha

Pampallaqta

Paru Paru

8520000

CU-112

8520000

Amaru

Uyucate

CU-112

Sacaca

Quello Quello

Chahuaytiri

CU-112

Chahuay

Pascanacancha

Kuyo Grande

CU-112

CU-112

CU-112

R19

13 29.0 S

Pukara Pantillijlla

72 09.0 W

R19

8515000

8515000

195000

200000

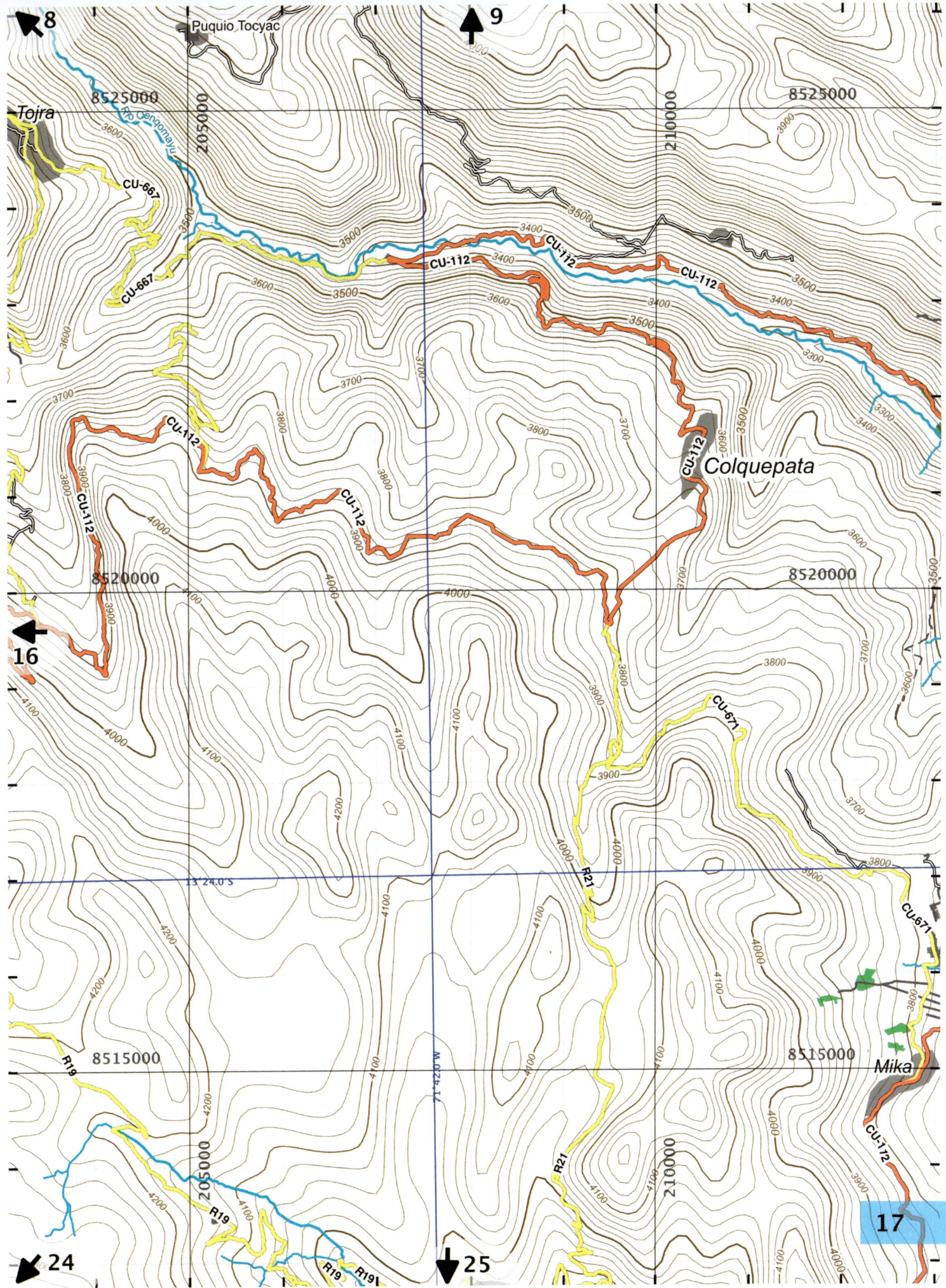

8 9

Puquio Tocyac

Tojra
8525000   8525000

CU-667

CU-667

CU-112   CU-112
CU-112   CU-112

CU-112

CU-112   CU-112

Colquepata

CU-112

16
8520000   8520000

CU-671

R21

13 24.0'S

CU-671

R19   8515000   8515000   Mika

R21

CU-112

R19

17

24   R19   R19   25

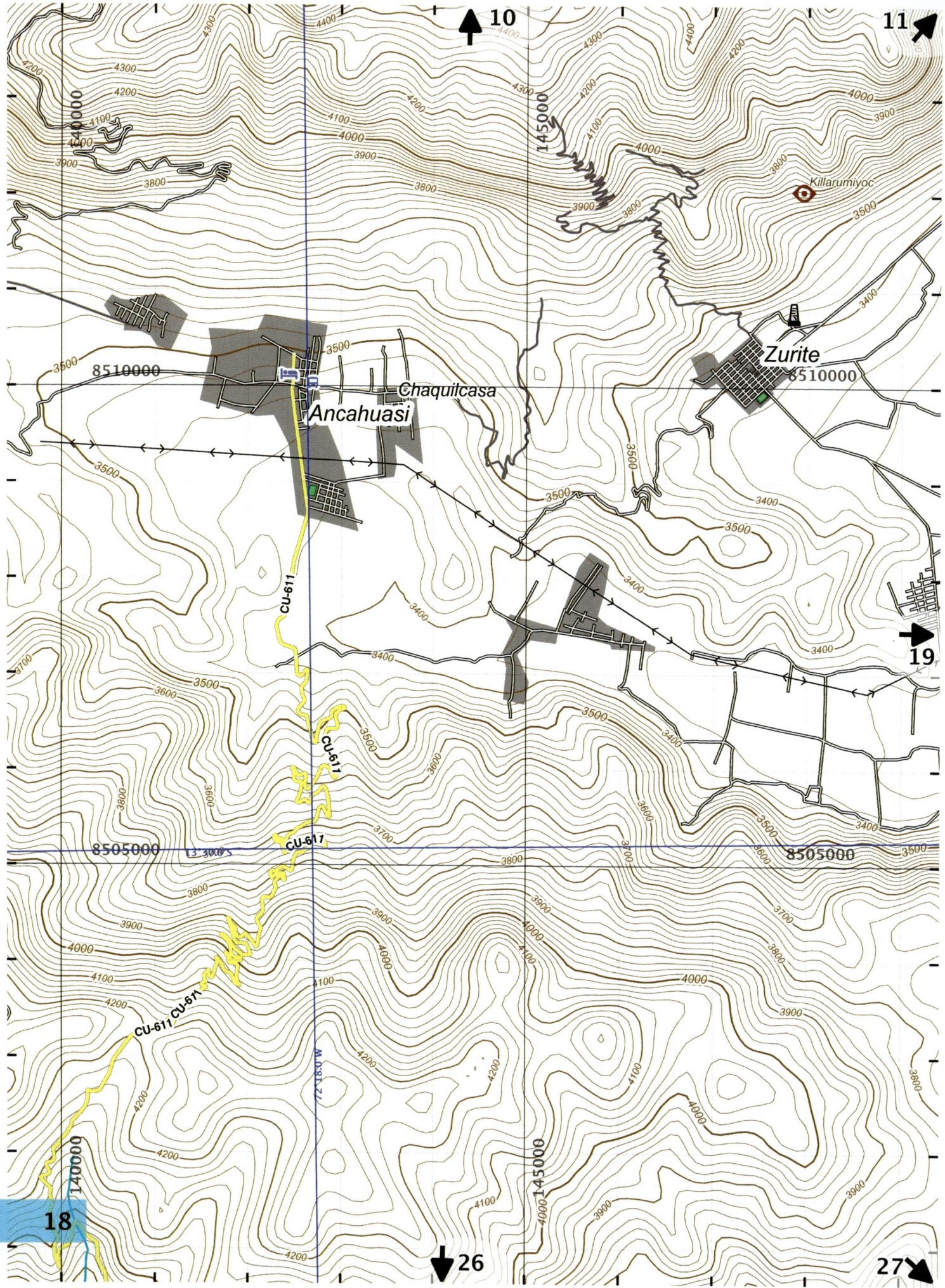

Killarumiyoc

Zurite

8510000

Chaquilcasa

Ancahuasi

8510000

CU-611

CU-611

CU-611

8505000

L 13 30'0"S

CU-611

8505000

W 72°18'0"

CU-611

CU-611

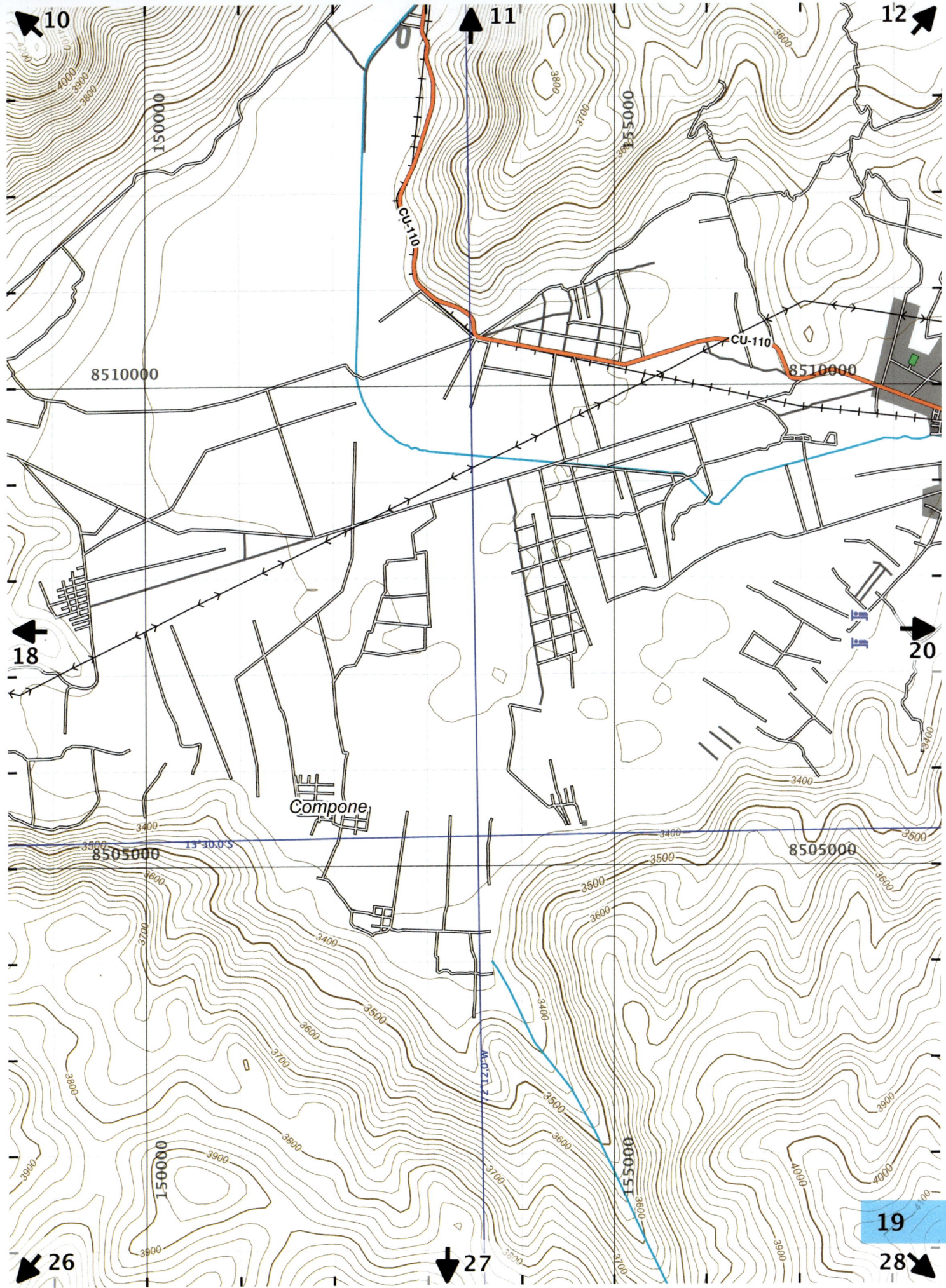

10
11
12
18
20
26
27
28
19

CU-110

CU-110

8510000

8510000

8505000

13 30.0 S

8505000

Compone

150000

150000

155000

155000

3600

3700

3800

3900

3400

3500

3600

3700

3900

4000

3600

3700

3800

3900

4000

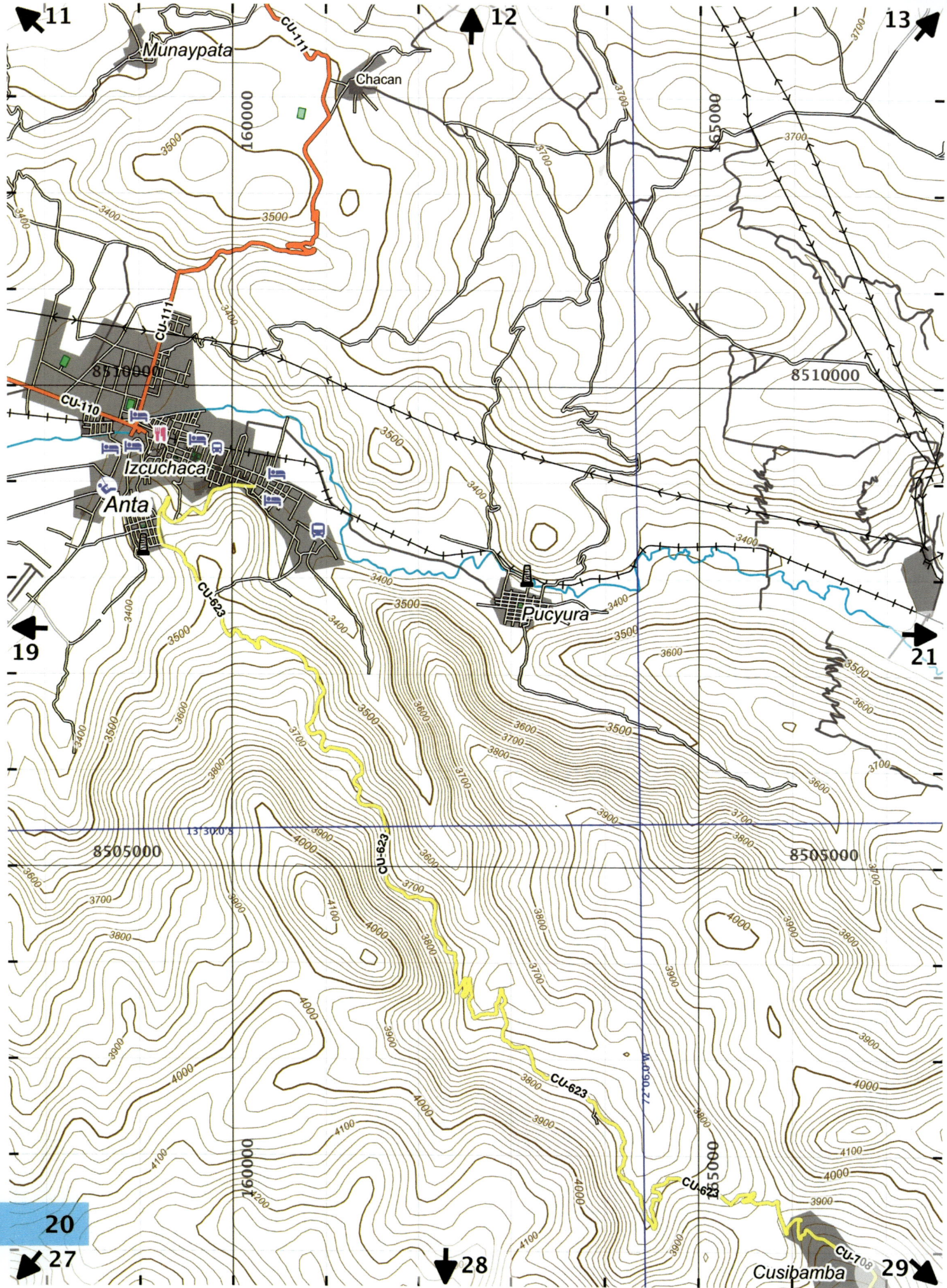

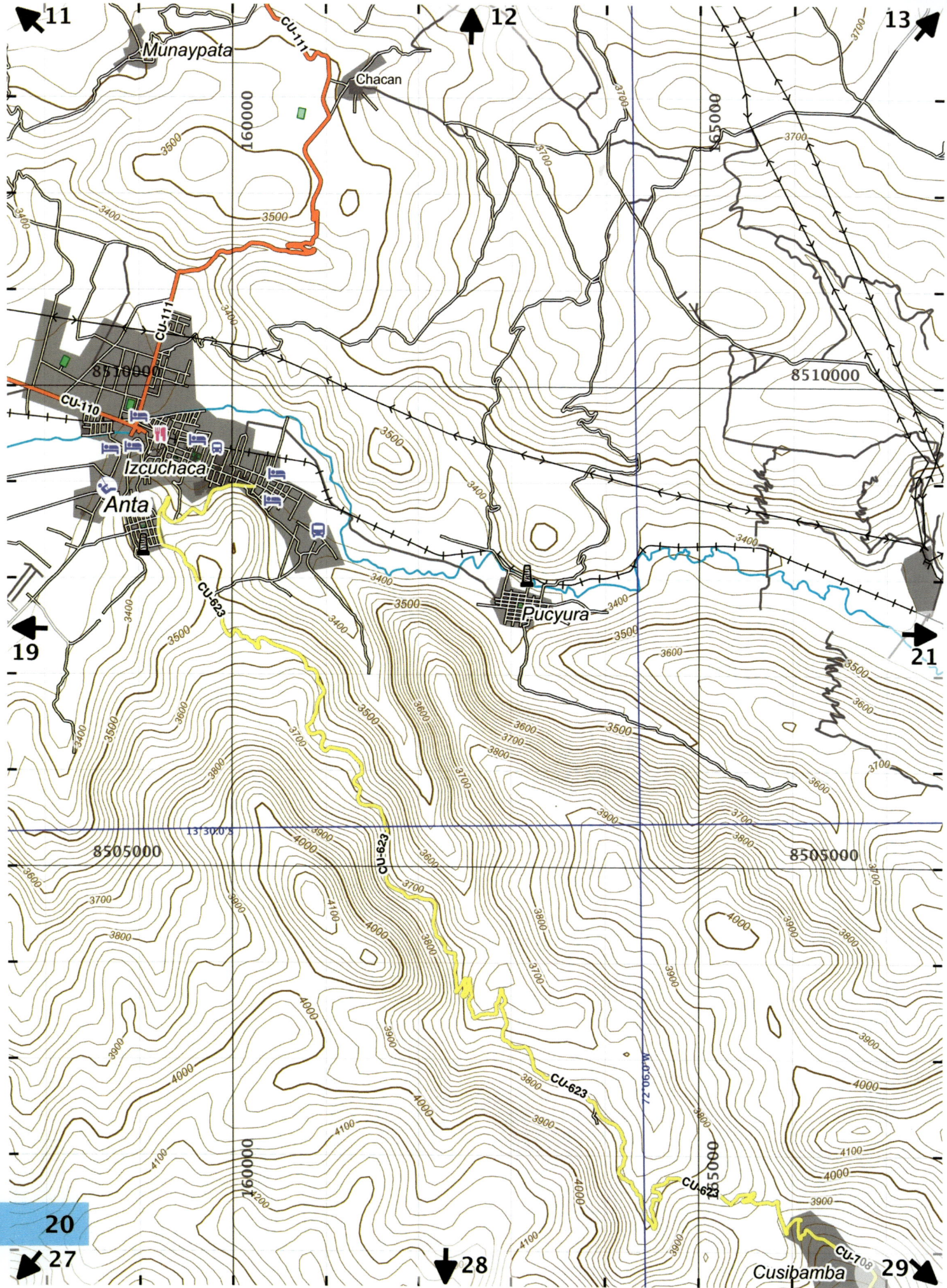

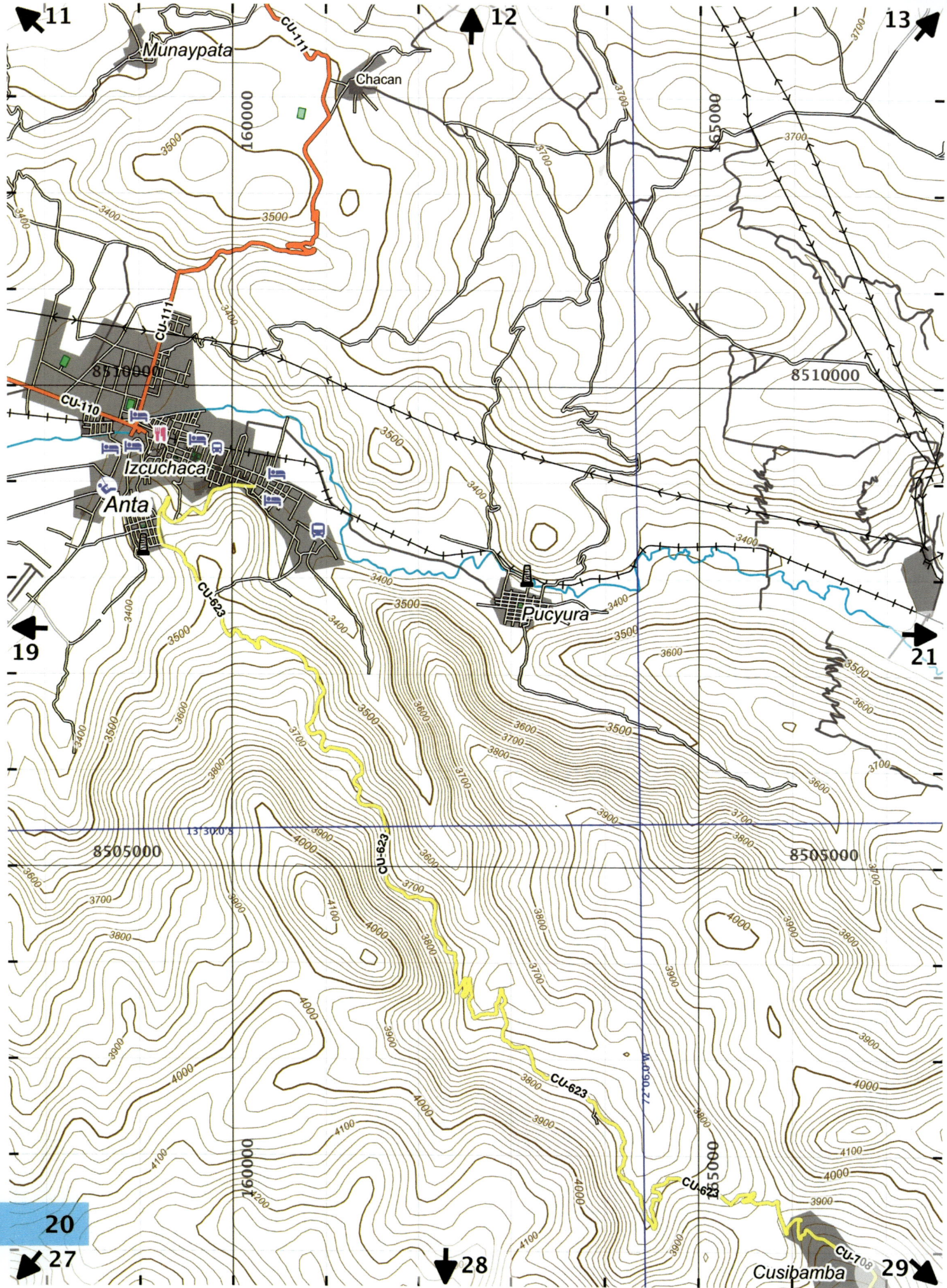

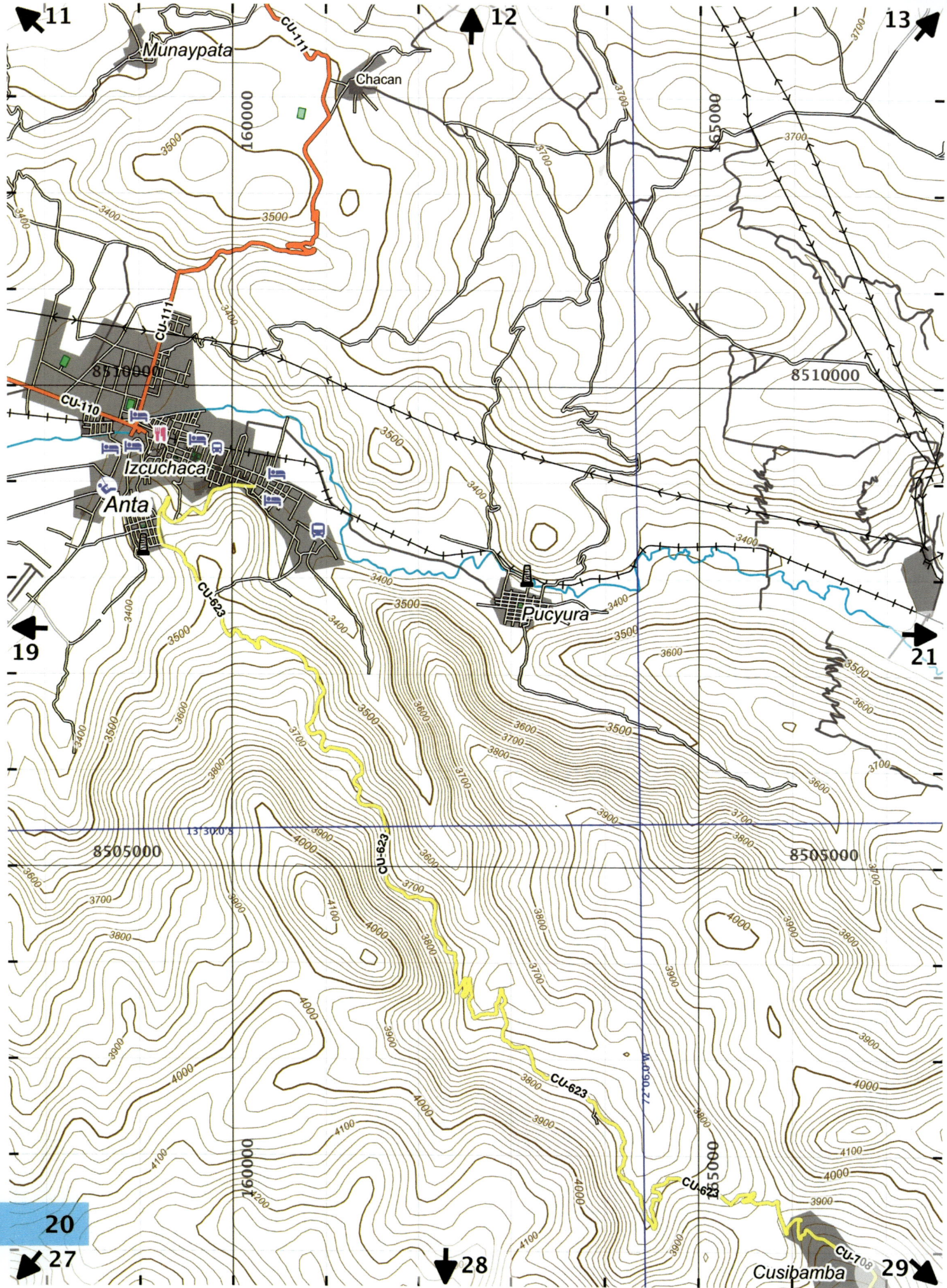

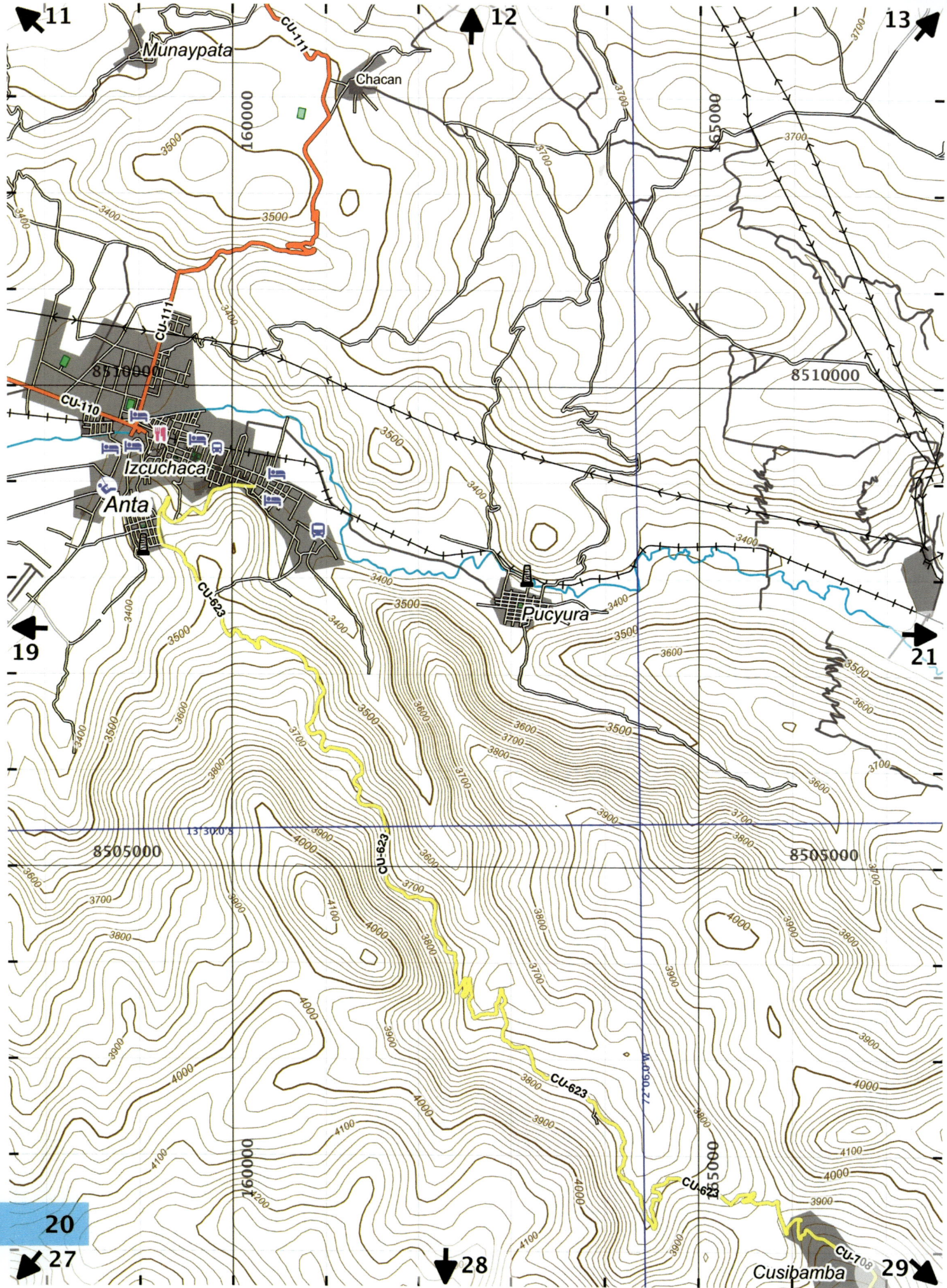

11

12

13

Munaypata

CU-111

Chacan

160000

3500

3500

3400

3500

3400

3700

3700

3700

65000

3700

8510000

8510000

CU-111

CU-110

Izcuchaca

Anta

3500

3400

3500

3400

3500

3400

Pucyura

3400

3500

3600

3500

3500

3600

19

21

3500

3600

3100

3600

13 30'0"S

3500

3600

3500

3700

3800

3700

3900

CU-623

8505000

8505000

3600

3700

3900

4000

3600

3800

3700

3800

3900

4000

3700

3800

CU-623

3900

4000

3900

4100

4000

3800

4100

3900

4000

4000

3900

3700

3800

3800

4000

CU-623

160000

20

27

28

29

Cusibamba

CU-7..8

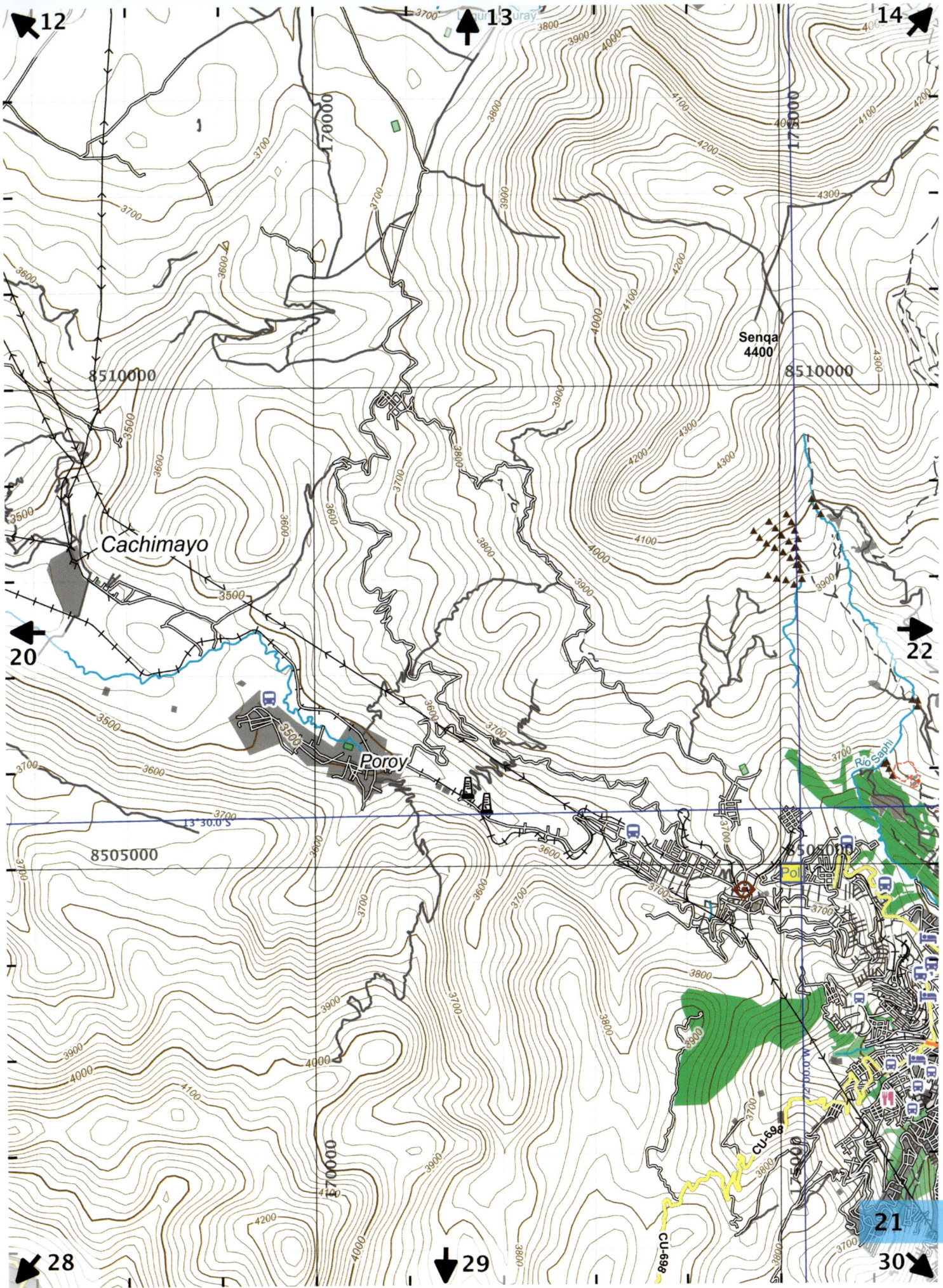

3700

3900
4000

4200

4300

4100

4200

4300

Senqa
4400

8510000

8510000

3700

3700

3600

3500

3500

3600

Cachimayo

3500

3800

3700

3600

4200

4300

4300

4100

4000

3900

3900

4000

4100

3800

3700

3600

3600

3500

3500

3700

3600

Poroy

3700

3600

3700

Río Saphi

3700

22

13 30.0' S

8505000

8505000

Pol

3700

3700

3800

3700

3800

3900

3700

3900

4000

3800

3900

4000

4100

4200

4100

3900

3800

3700

CU-698

4000

4100

CU-698

3800

3700

3800

3700

21

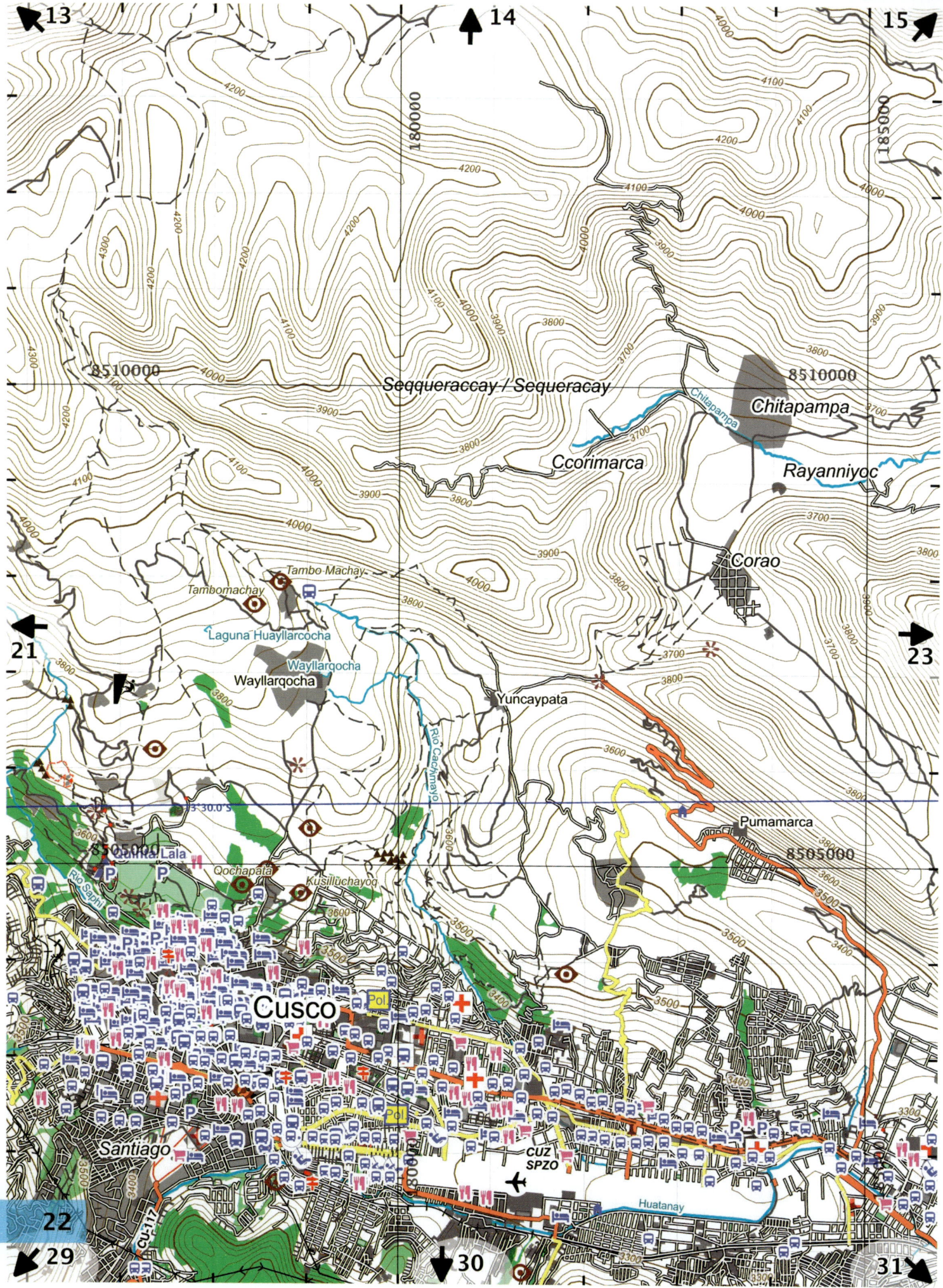

180000

185000

8510000

Seqqueraccay / Sequeracay

8510000

Chitapampa

Chitapampa

Ccorimarca

Rayanniyoc

Corao

Tambo Machay

Tambomachay

Laguna Huayllarcocha

Wayllarqocha

Wayllarqocha

Yuncaypata

Río Cachimayo

Pumamarca

8505000

8505000

13°30.0'S

Quinta Lala

Qochapata

Kusiluchayoq

Río Saphi

Cusco

Pol

Pol

Santiago

CUZ
SPZO

CUZ-117

Huatanay

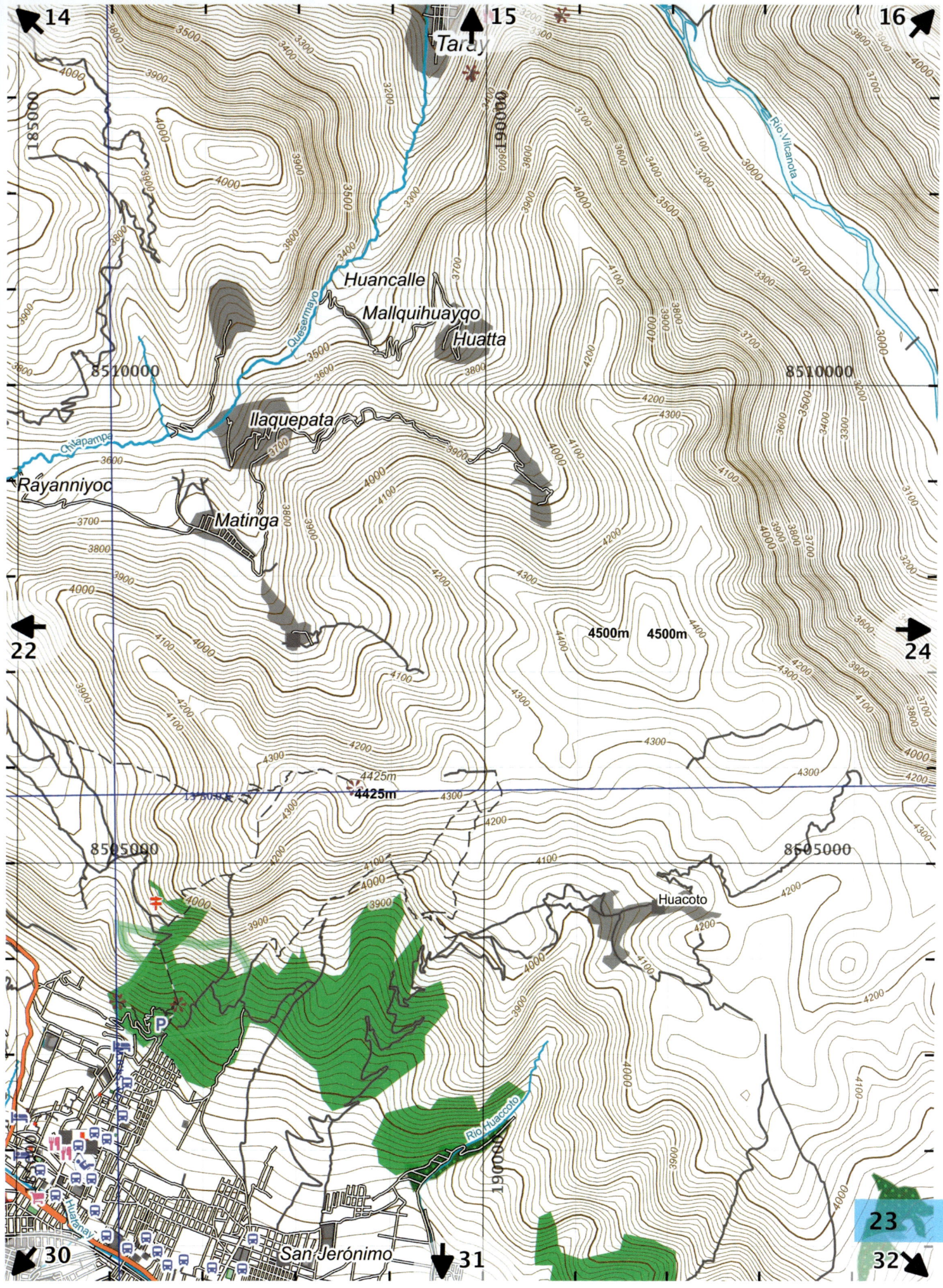

Taray

Río Vilcanota

18590000

Huancalle

Mallquihuayqo

Huatta

8510000 8510000

Quesermayo

Ilaquepata

Chivapampa

Rayanniyoc

3700

Matinga

4500m 4500m

4425m

4425m

8505000 8505000

Huacoto

P

Río Huaccolo

San Jerónimo

Huatanay

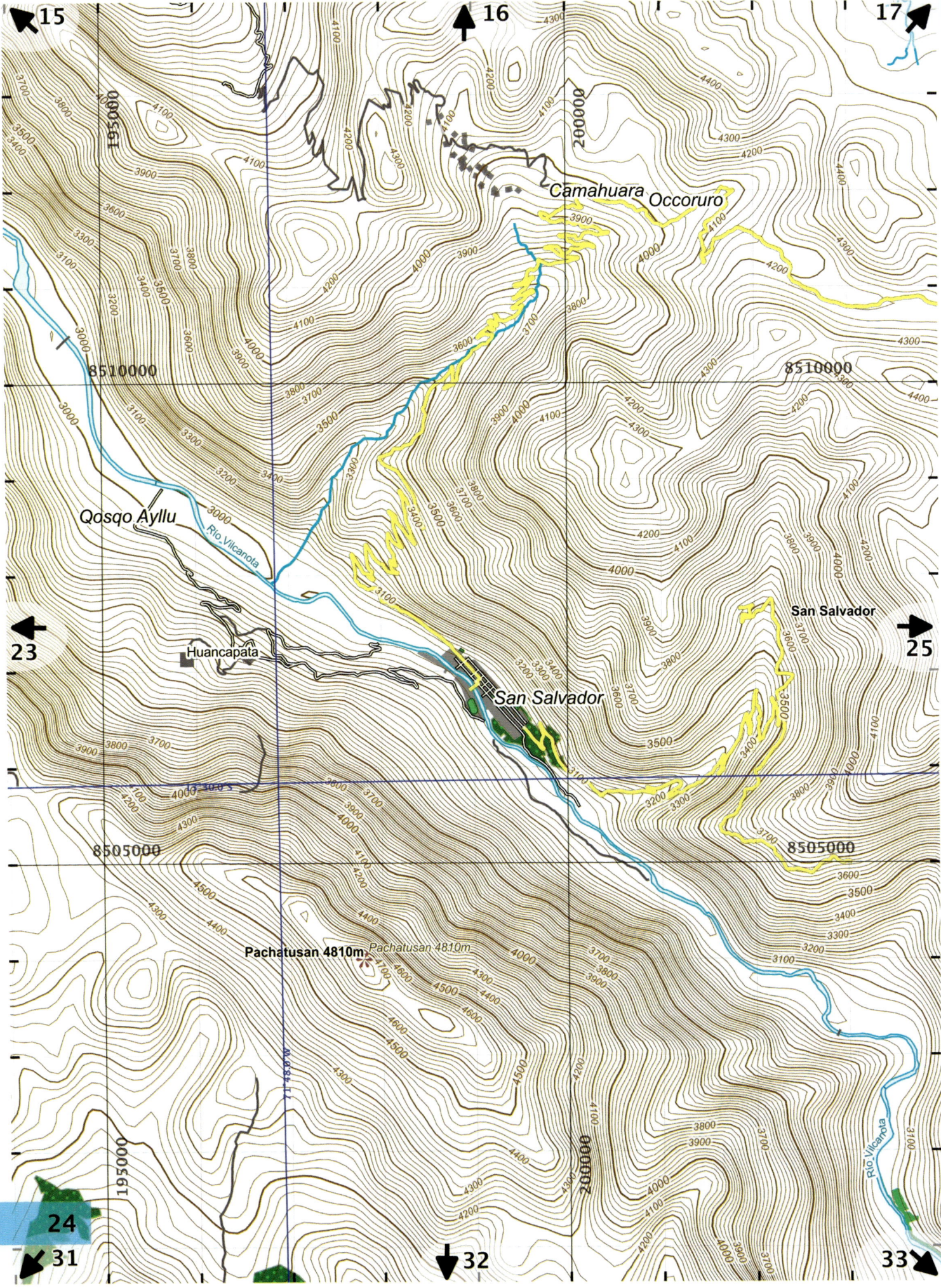

200000

195000

8510000

8510000

Camahuara *Occoruro*

Qosqo Ayllu

Rio Vilcanota

San Salvador

Huancapata

San Salvador

8505000

8505000

Pachatusan 4810m *Pachatusan 4810m*

190000

200000

Rio Vilcanota

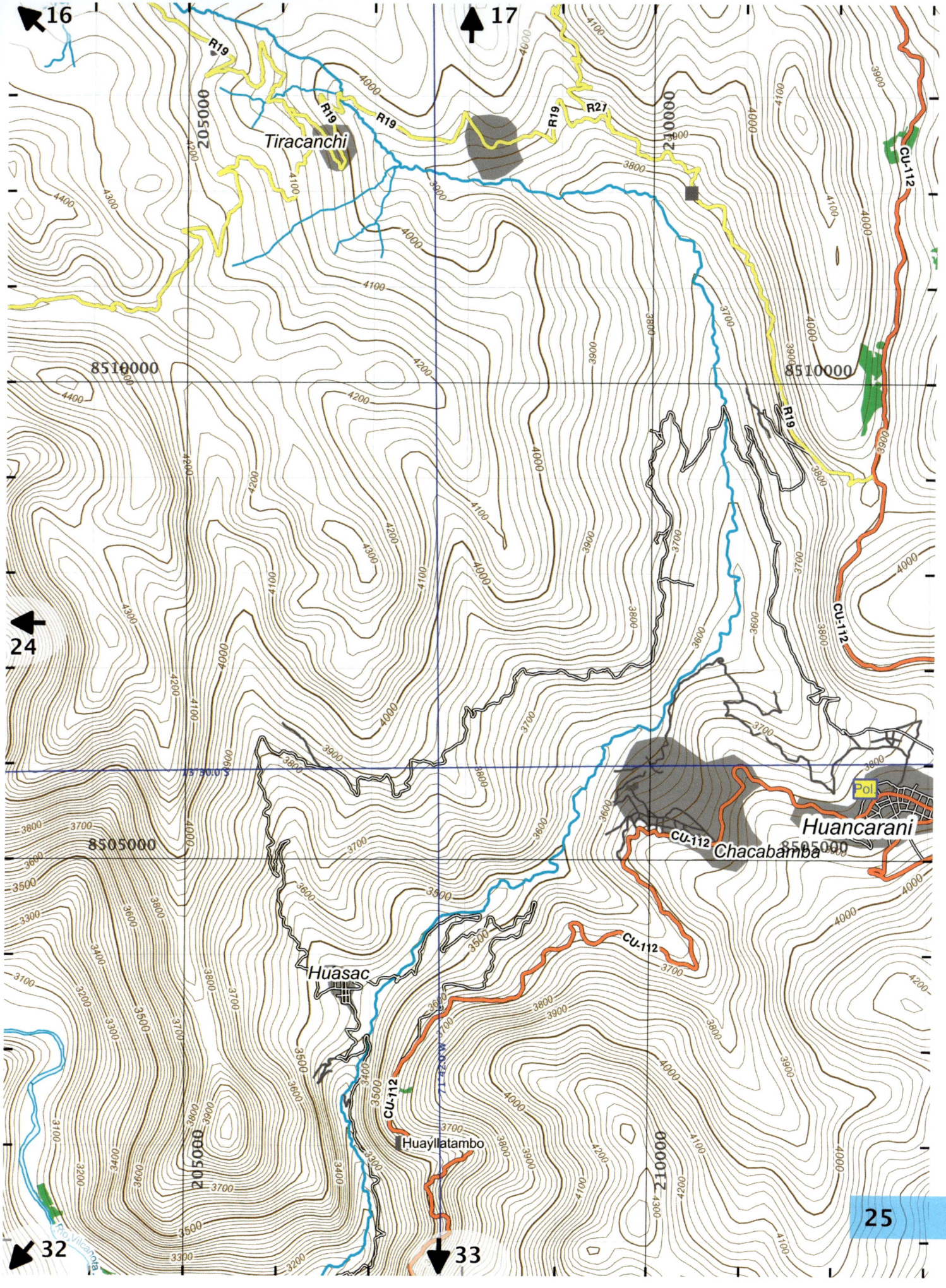

R19
R19
R19
R19
R27
R19

CU-112

Tiracanchi

205000
210000
8510000
8510000

R19

CU-112

CU-112

Pol

Huancarani

8505000
8505000
Chacabamba

CU-112

Huasac

CU-112

CU-112

13°50.0'S

Huayllatambo

72°42.0'W

205000
210000

Lago Vilcanota

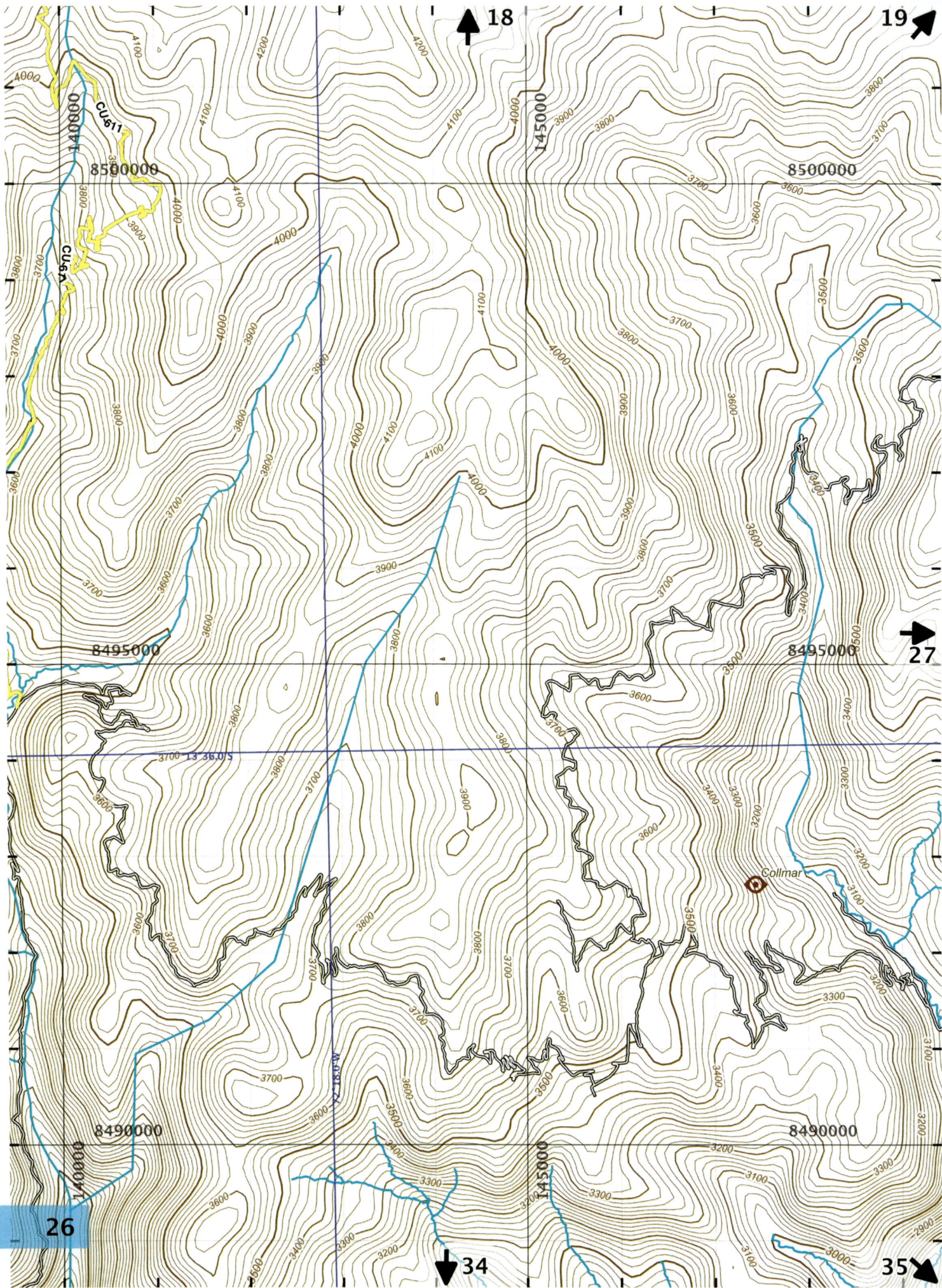

CU 611

CU 6A

145000

8500000

8500000

8495000

8495000

27

3700 13 36.0 S

Collmar

8490000

8490000

145000

170000

34

35

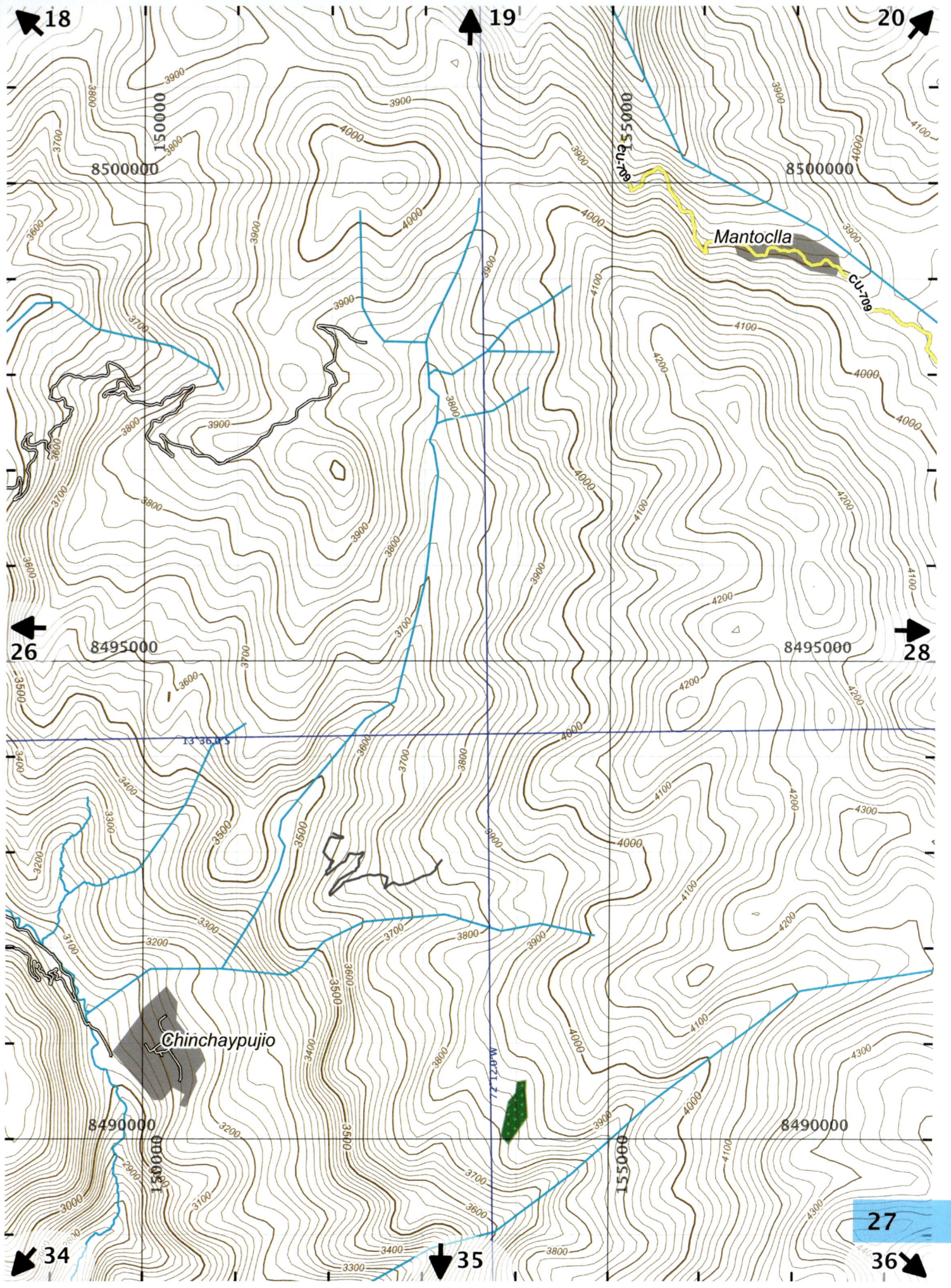

150000

8500000

Mantoclla

cu-709

8500000

3900

4000

4100

4200

4300

26

8495000

8495000

28

13°36'0"S

72°12'0"W

Chinchaypujio

8490000

8490000

155000

150000

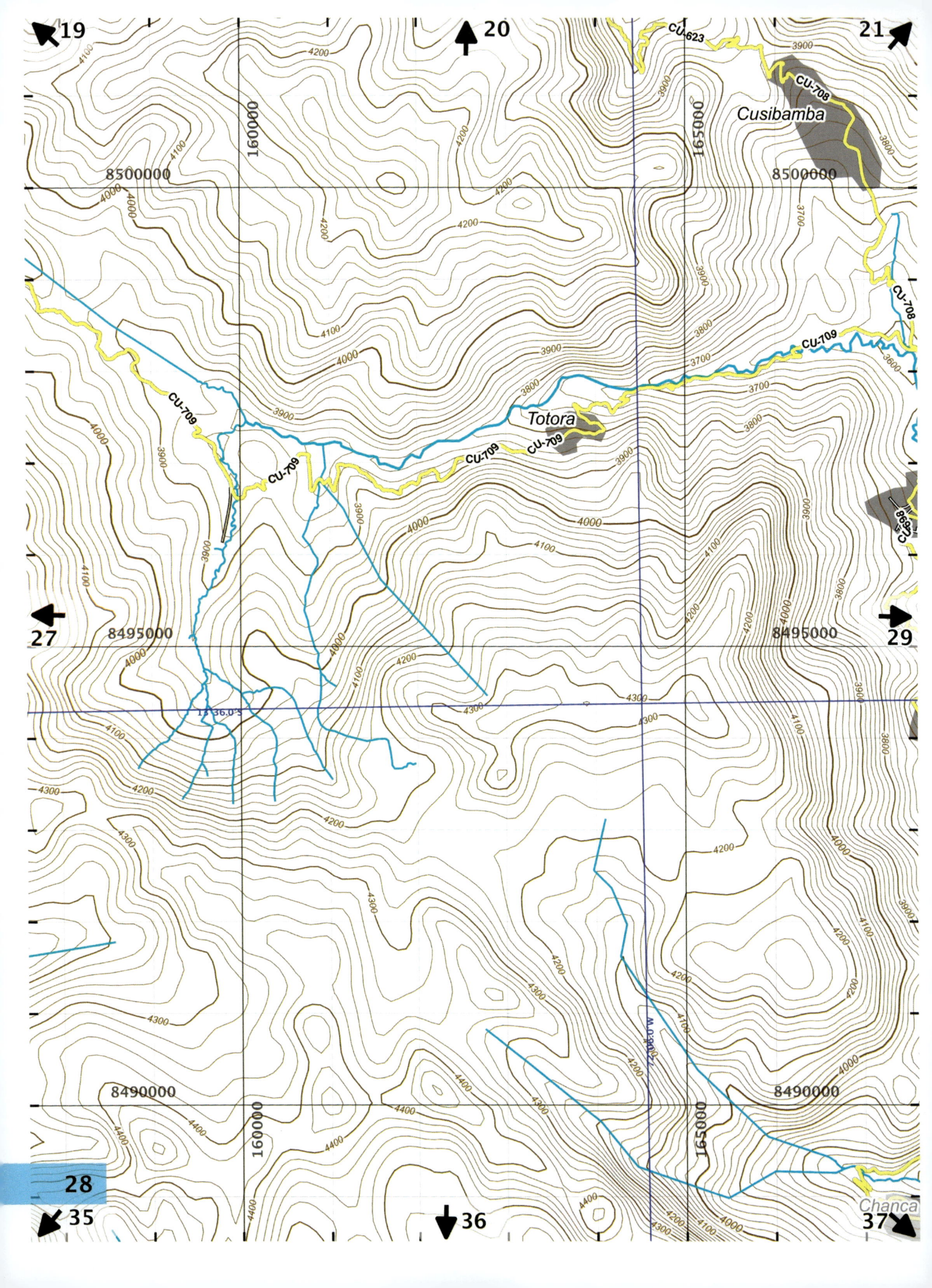

CU-623

CU-708

Cusibamba

CU-708

CU-709

8500000

8500000

CU-709

CU-709

Totora

CU-709 CU-709

CU-709

8495000

8495000

160000

160500

13°36.0'S

4300

4300

8490000

8490000

160000

160500

Chanca

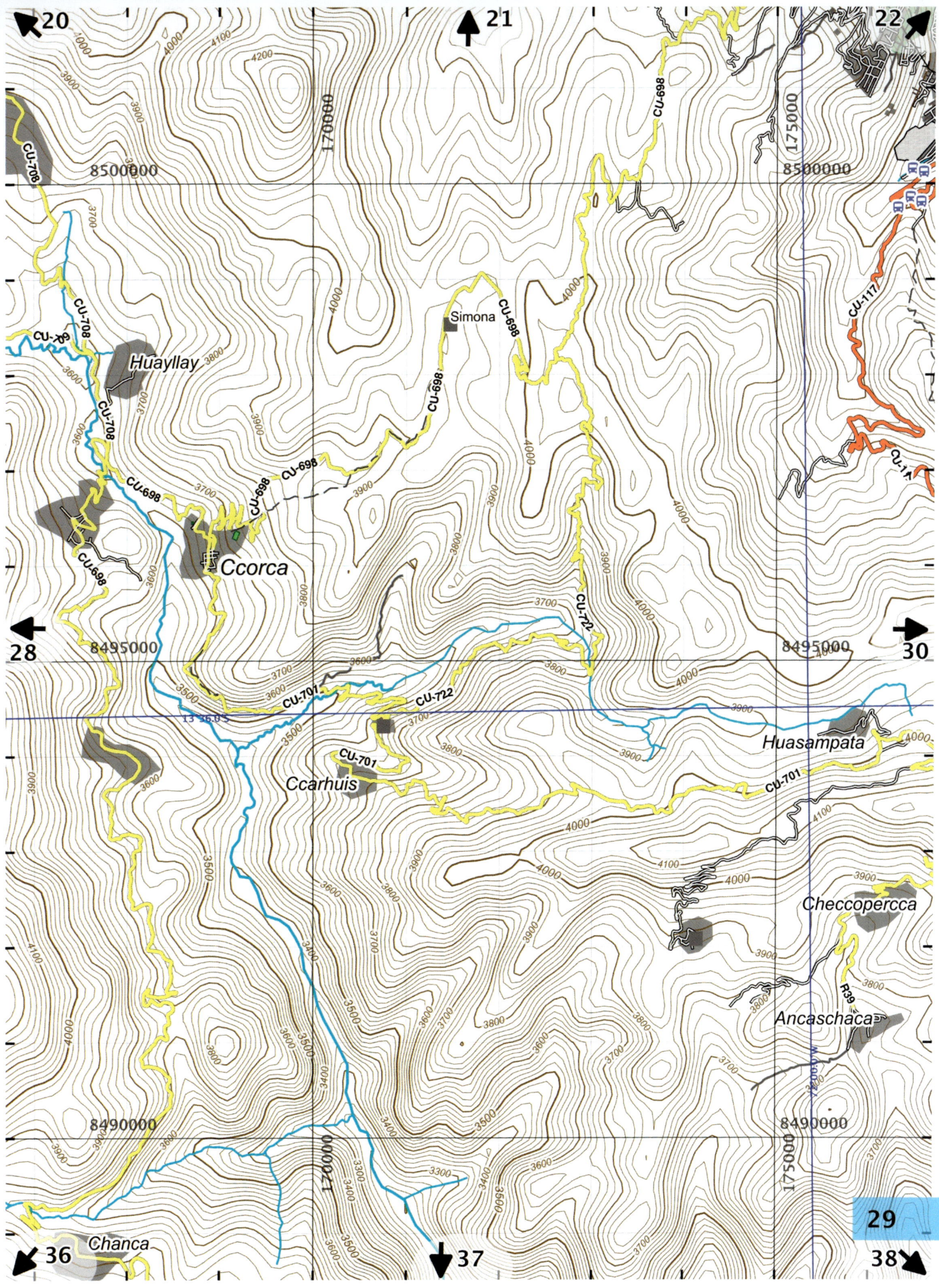

CU-708

8500000

CU-708

CU-698

175000

170000

CU-R9

CU-708

Huayllay

CU-708

Simona

CU-698

CU-698

CU-117

CU-698

CU-1A

CU-698

Ccorca

CU-698

8495000

CU-722

CU-701

8495000

13 36.0 S

CU-722

Huasampata

CU-701

CU-701

Ccarhuis

Checcopercca

R39

175000

170000

Ancaschaca

8490000

8490000

Chanca

29

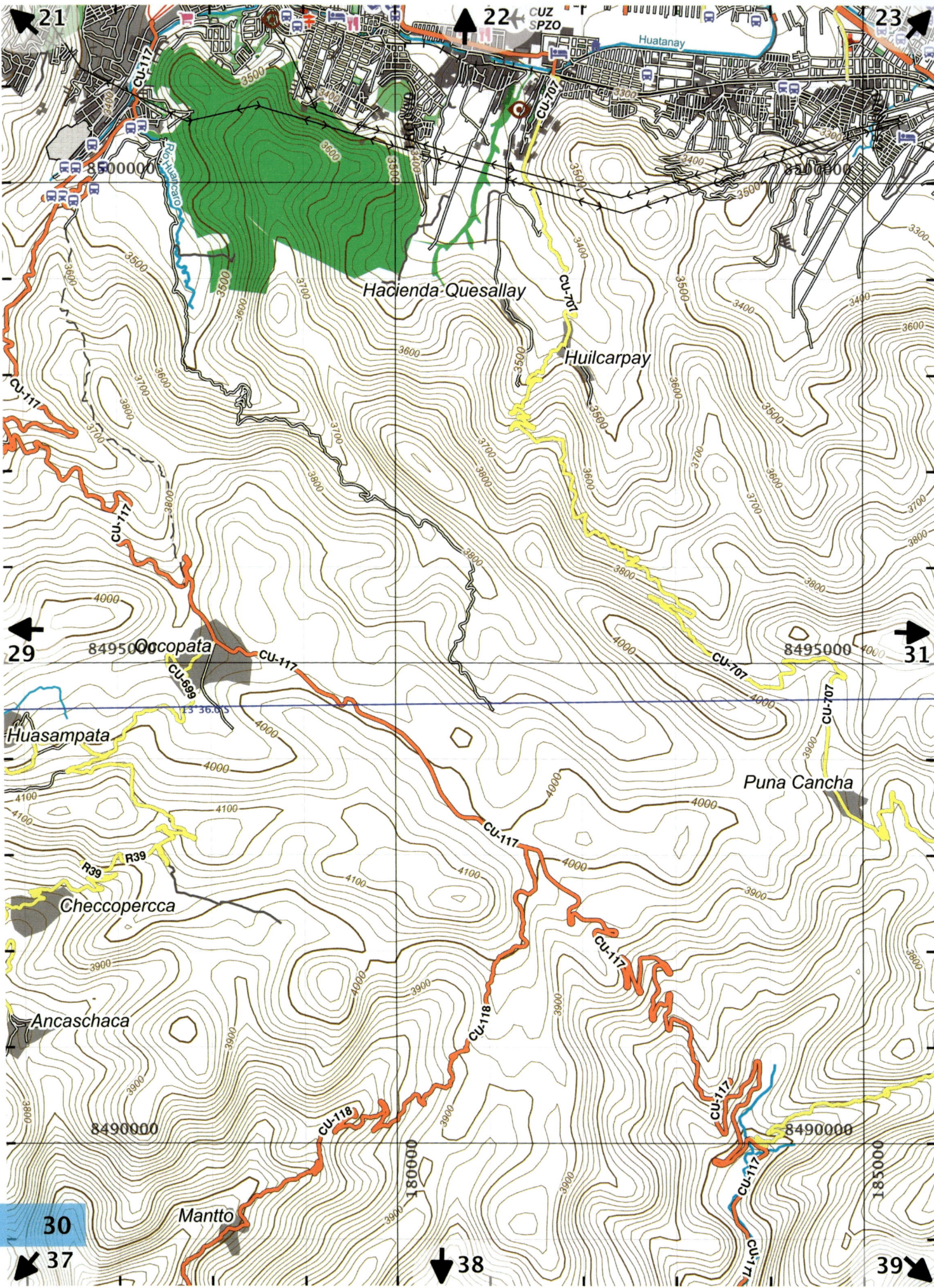

CUZ
SPZO

Huatanay

CU-117

Río Huancaro

8500000

3500

3600

3700

3500

CU-707

Hacienda Quesallay

Huilcarpay

CU-707

3600

3700

3800

3500

3600

3700

3800

CU-117

3700

3800

3900

4000

8495000
Occopata
CU-117
CU-699

CU-117
CU-707
8495000

Puna Cancha

CU-707

13 36.6 S

Huasampata

4000

4100

R39 R39

Checcopercca

CU-117

CU-117

CU-118

4100

4000

3900

CU-117

CU-117

Ancaschaca

3900

CU-117

8490000
CU-118

8490000

180000

185000

Mantto

CU-118

CU-117

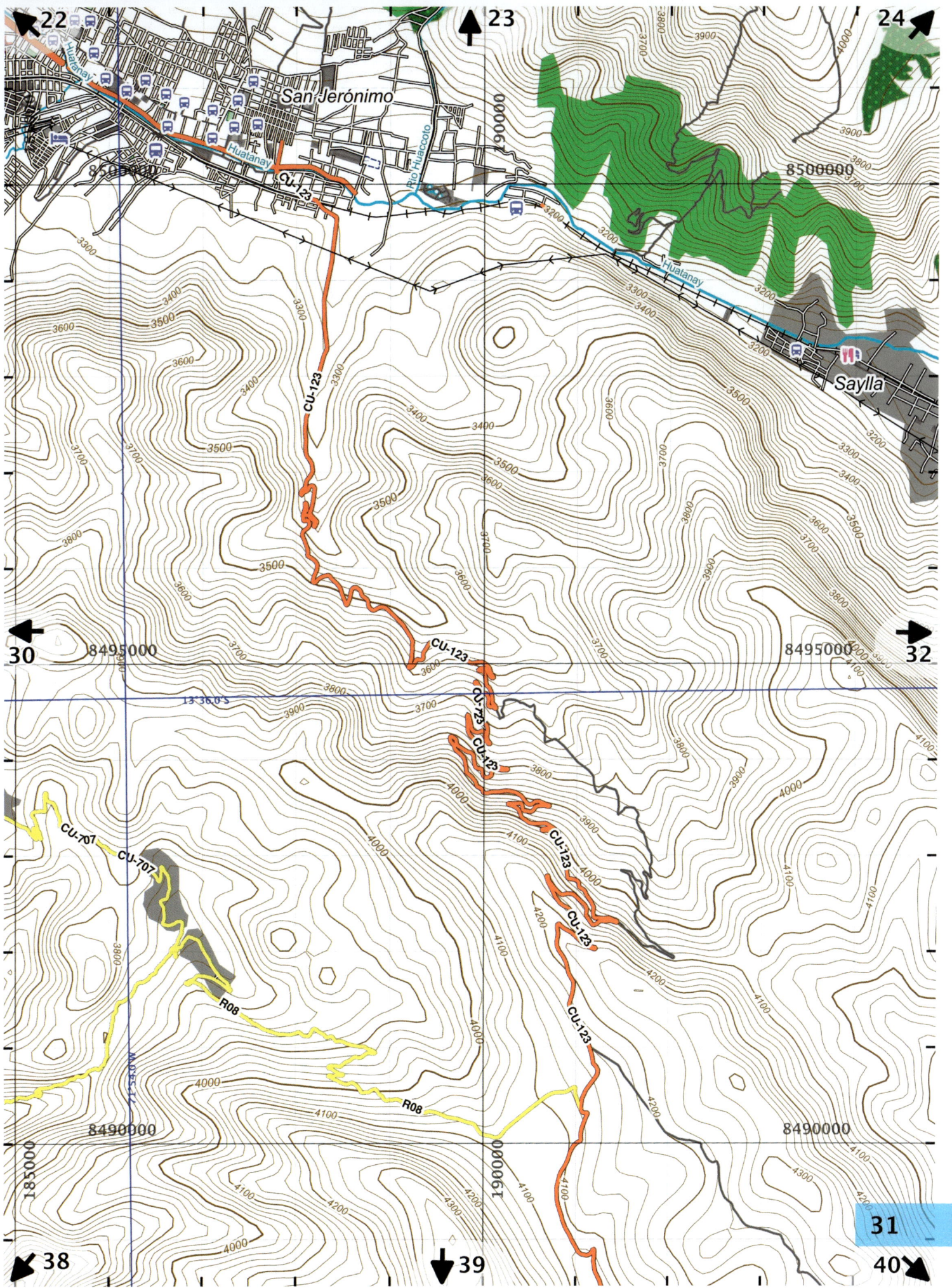

San Jerónimo

Huatanay

Río Huáccoto

CU-123

8500000

Huatanay

8500000

3900

3800

3700

3200

3300

3400

3500

3600

3700

3800

Saylla

CU-123

3600
3500
3400
3300
3500
3600
3700
3800
3700

3400
3500
3600

3500

CU-123

8495000

8495000

13°36.0'S

3800

3900

3700

CU-123

CU-123

CU-123

4000

CU-707

CU-707

R08

4000

4100

4200

CU-123

CU-123

CU-123

4100

4000

4200

R08

8490000

8490000

185000

190000

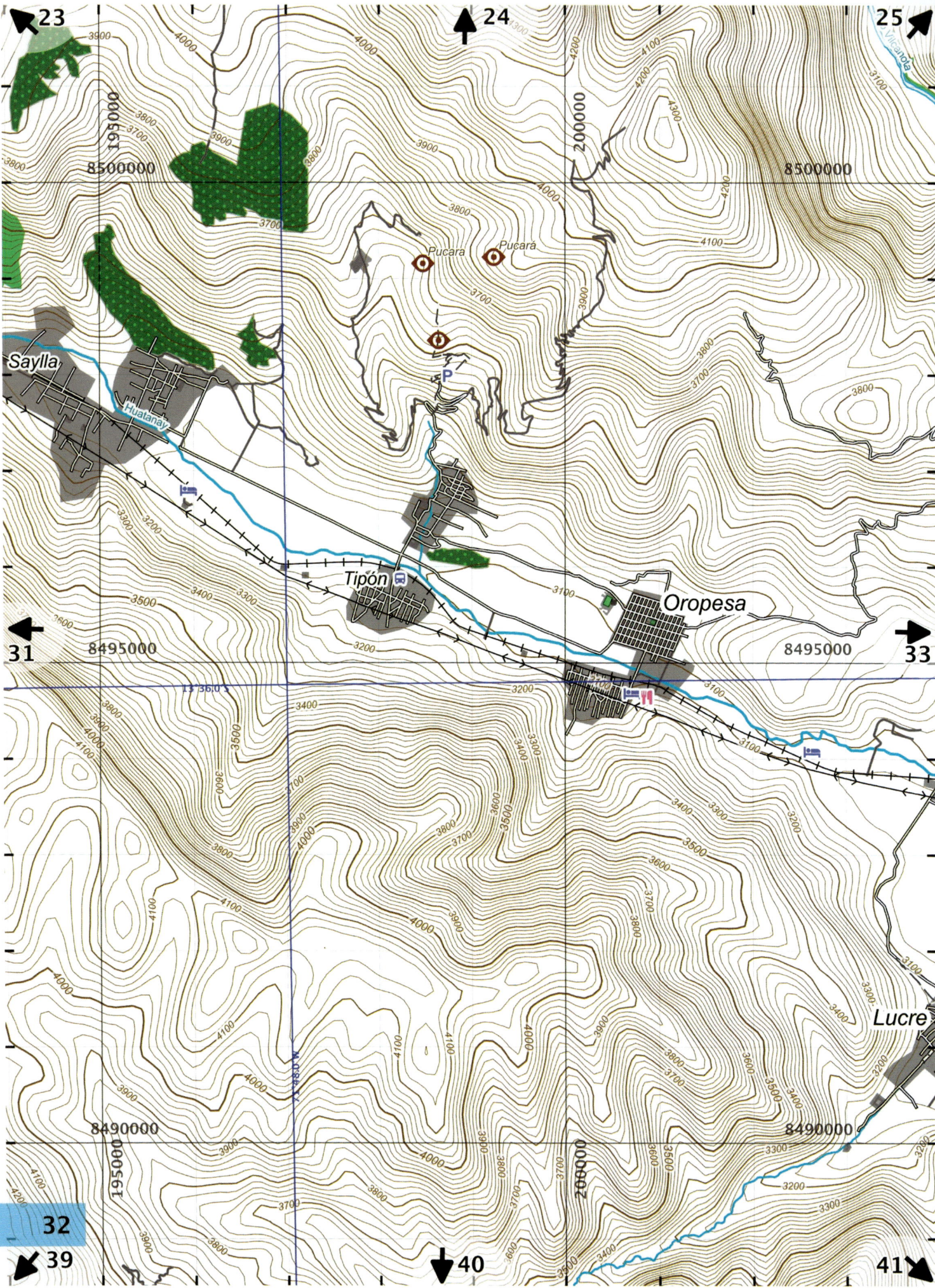

195000

8500000

200000

8500000

3900
4000
4000
4100
4200
4300
4100
3900
3800
3800
3700
3900
4000
3800
3700

Pucara
Pucará

3700

P

Saylla

Huatanay

3300
3200
3500
3400
3300

Tipón

3100

Oropesa

8495000
8495000

3200
3400
3300

3100

3400

4000
4100

3800
3500
3600
3700
3800

3600
3700

3800

3500
3400
3300

Lucre

195000
8490000
200000
8490000

3900
4000
4100
3800
3700
3600
3500
3400
3300
3200

3300

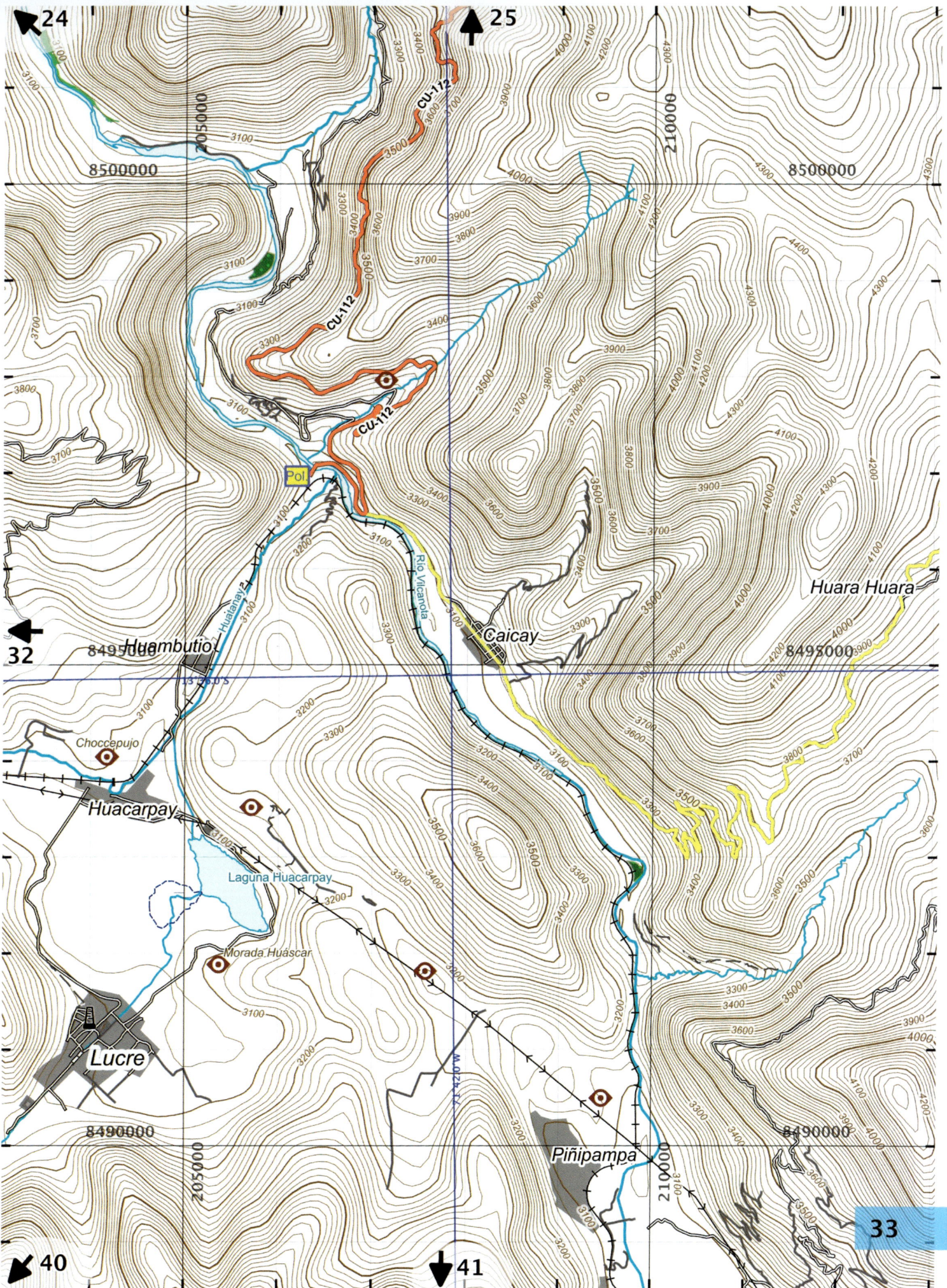

CU-112

8500000

205000

210000

8500000

CU-112

CU-112

Pol.

CU-112

Río Vilcanota

Huara Huara

8495000

Huambutío

Caicay

8495000

13°30'S

Choccepujo

Huacarpay

Laguna Huacarpay

Morada Huáscar

Lucre

8490000

8490000

205000

210000

Piñipampa

72°30'W

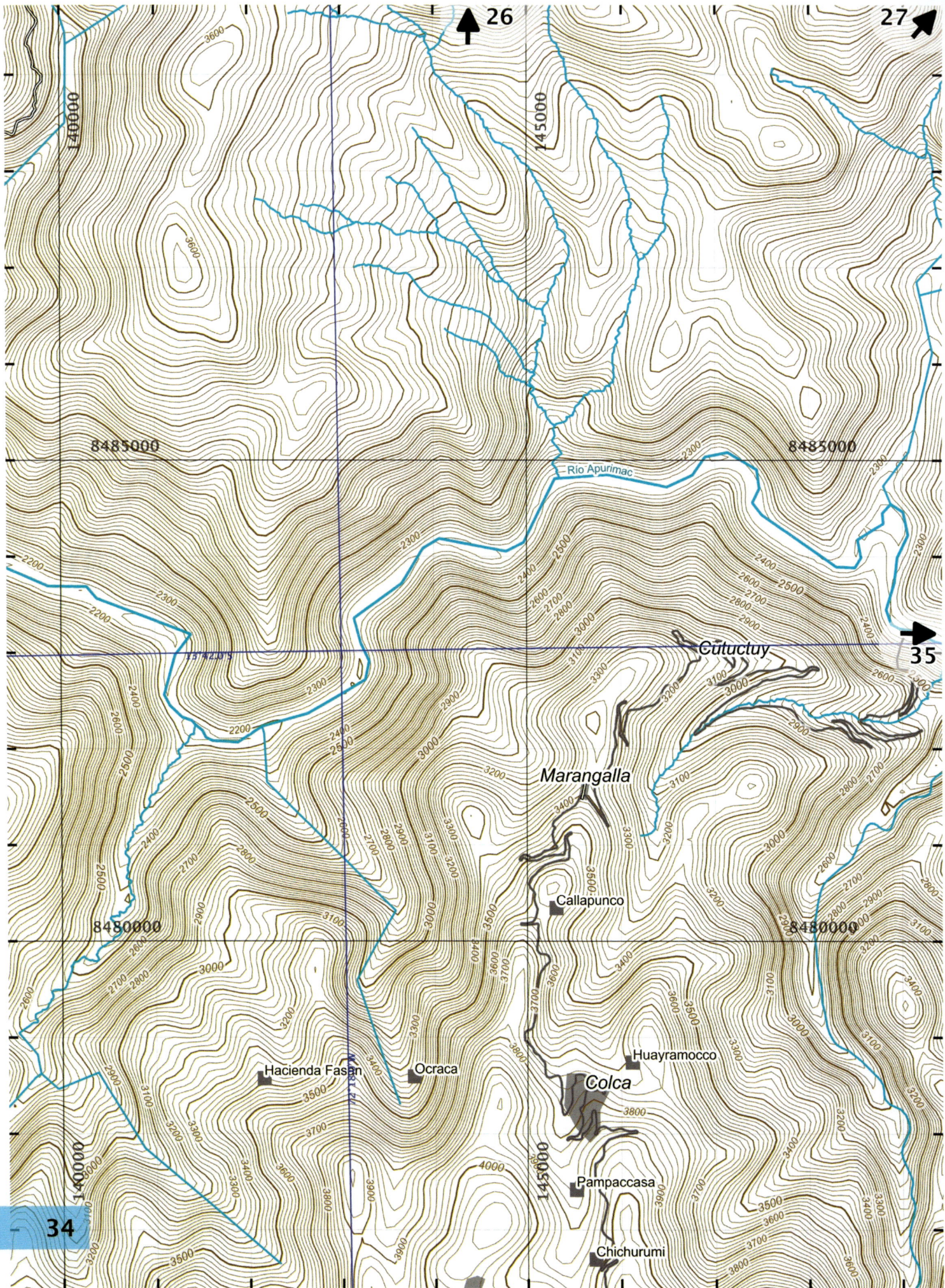

8485000

8485000

Río Apurímac

Cutuctuy

Marangalla

Callapunco

8480000

8480000

Huayramocco

Hacienda Fasan

Ocraca

Colca

Pampaccasa

Chichurumi

150000

3800
3900
3600
3400
3300
3200
3100
3000
2900
2800
2700
2600
2500
2400

4100
4400
4300
4200
4000

155000

8485000   8485000

3700
3600
3500
3400
3300
3200
3100
3000

3900
3800
3700
3600
3500

34   36

Rallarqui

Aravito

Río Apurimac

2900
2800
2700
2600
2500
2400
2300

3100
3000

8480000   8480000

3400

150000

155000

Pamparqui

Chahuarqui

Chanca

160000

165000

8485000

8485000

35

37

8480000

8480000

CU-118
CU-118
CU-118

160000

165000

Río Apurímac

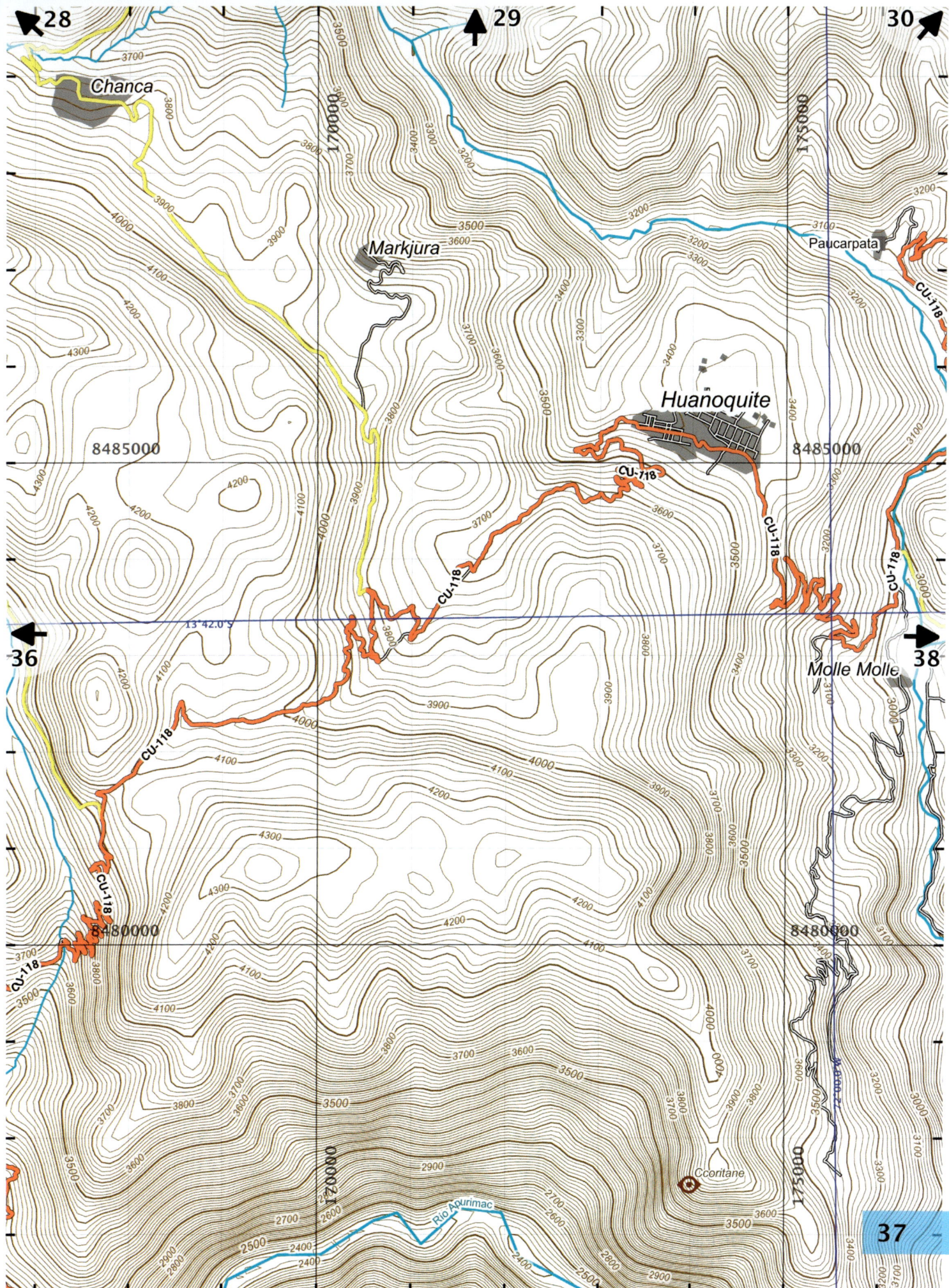

Chanca

3700

3800

3900

4000

4100

4200

4300

Markjura

3600

3500

3400

3300

3200

3100

Paucarpata

CU-118

3200

Huanoquite

3400

CU-118

8485000

8485000

CU-118

3700

3600

CU-118

4200

4100

4000

3900

3800

3500

CU-118

13° 42.0' S

Molle Molle

CU-118

4000

4100

4300

4200

CU-118

CU-118

8480000

8480000

4100

4200

4300

Ccoritane

Río Apurimac

2900

2800

2700

2600

2500

2400

Mantto

CU-118

Parpay

Paucarpata

CU-118

Chifya Amaru

Sayhuacalla

Yaurisque

CU-117

CU-117

CU-117

8485000

8485000

CU-118

Tarurpay

Maucallacta

Puma Orco

Molle Molle

Mollebamba

Rumiticte

Ccarhuaccalla

CU-119

8480000

8480000

CU-119

Paccaritambo

CU-119

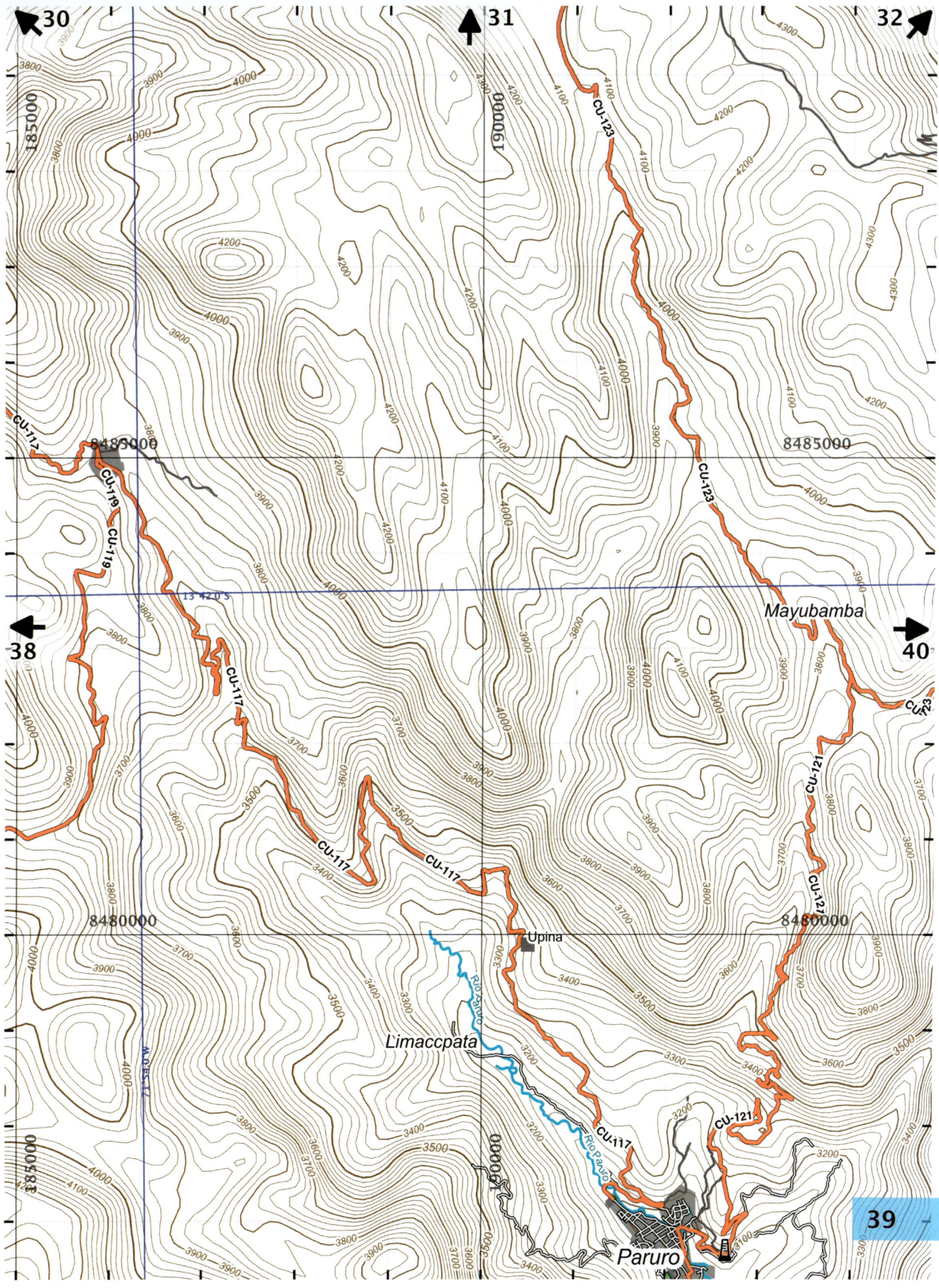

CU-123

CU-123

8485000

8485000

Mayubamba

CU-117

CU-119

CU-119

CU-117

13°42'0"S

CU-121

CU-123

CU-117

CU-117

CU-121

8480000

8480000

Upina

Río Apurío

CU-121

Limaccpata

Río Paruro

CU-117

71°50'0"W

Paruro

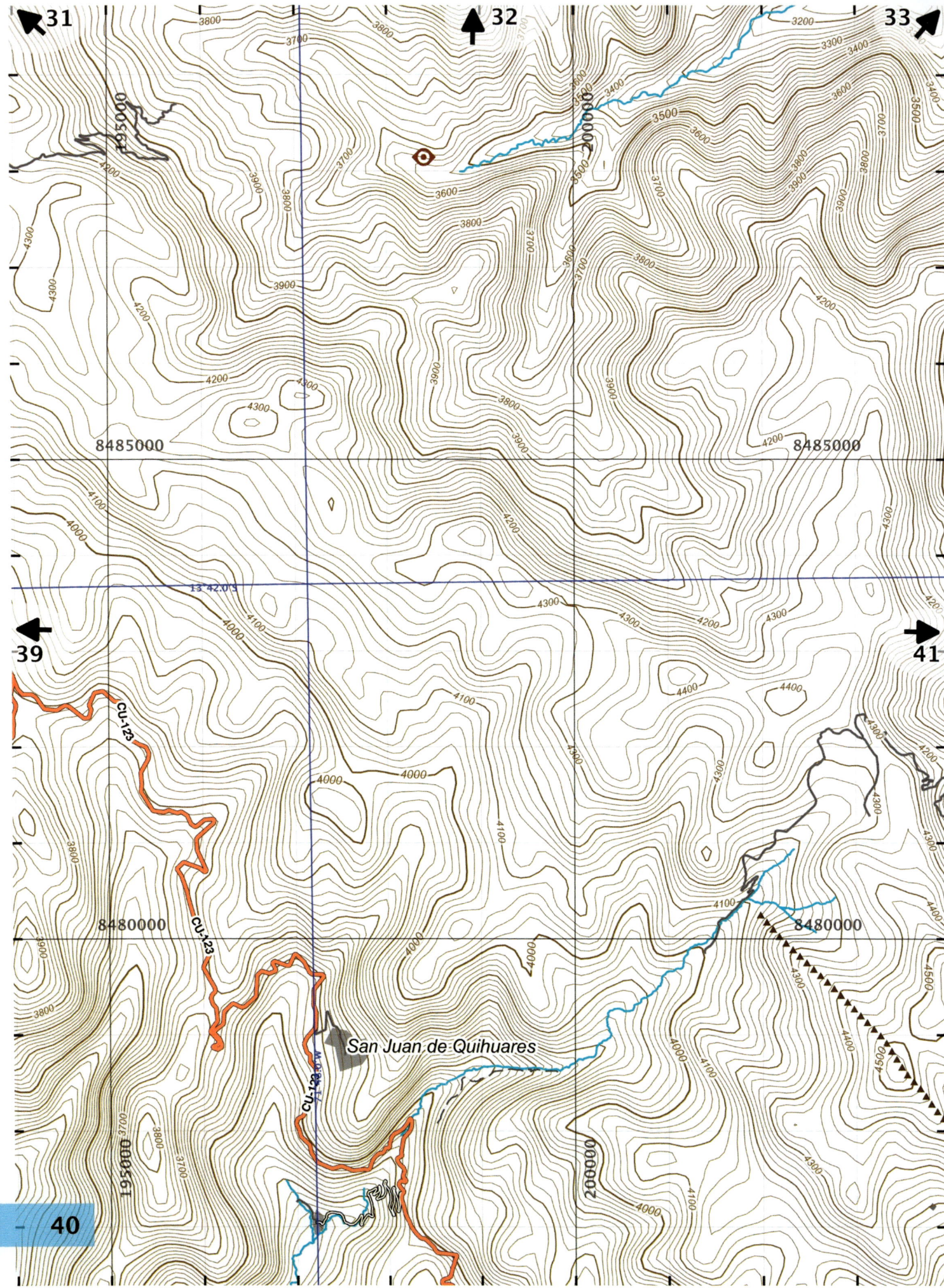

3800
3700
3800
3200
3400

3500
3600
3700
3800
3900

3900
3800
3600
3700

4300
4200
4300
3900

3800
4200
4300

8485000
8485000

4200
4300
4000
4100

4200
4300

13 42.00

4300
4300
4200
4300
4200

CU-123
4000
4000
4400
4400
4300

4000
4100
4300

8480000
CU-123
4000
4100
8480000

3800
4500

3800
3700
San Juan de Quihuares
4000
4100
4300
4400

CU-123
3800
3700
4100
4000

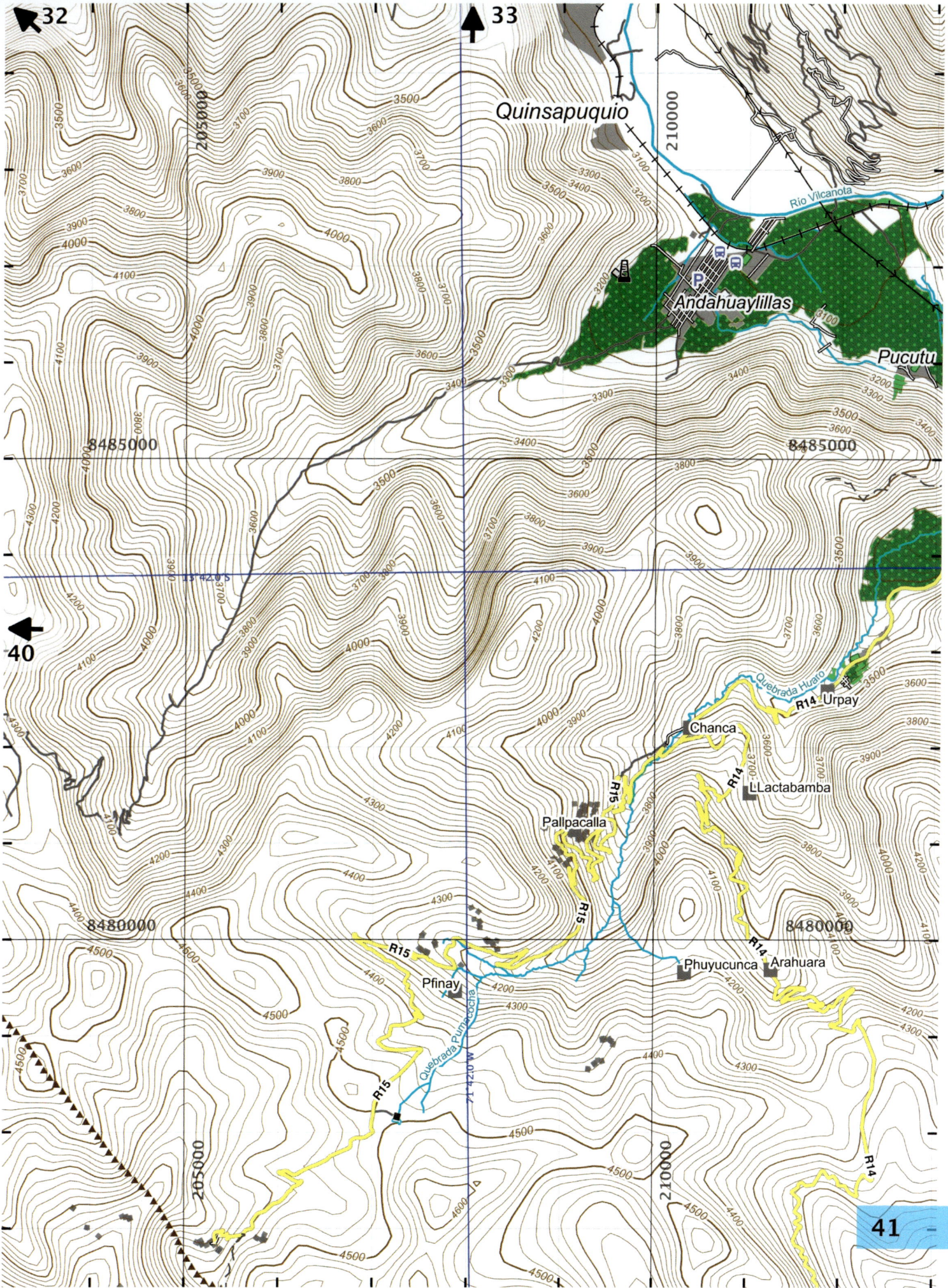

Quinsapuquio

210000

Río Vilcanota

Andahuaylillas

Pucutu

8485000

8485000

40

13°42'0"S

Quebrada Huaro

R14 Urpay

Chanca

R15

LLactabamba

R14

Pallpacalla

R15

8480000

8480000

R15

Phuyucunca

Arahuara

R14

Pfinay

Quebrada Puña-cocha

71°42'0"W

R15

R14

205000

210000

Map & Atlas Design Copyright © Sergio Mazitto Topo Maps, 2018

Some map data Copyright © Openstreetmap contributors

Published by Sergio Mazitto

26018330R00026

Printed in Poland
by Amazon Fulfillment
Poland Sp. z o.o., Wrocław